Pride: Good and Bad

Christian Theology Series

Robert Lloyd Russell

Published by LCL Company NW, 2022.

Also by Robert Lloyd Russell

Bible Character Series
Samson: Spirit-Controlled to Self-Centered
Peter: Failure to Faith

Christian Concepts Series
God's Church: Christ's Pearl
God's Nature: Sonlight Sunlight
God's Child: Like a Tree

Christian Growth Series
God's Desire: How To Please God
God's Light: How To Respond
Christ's Disciple: How To Finish Strong

Christian Theology Series
Christ's Blood: 7+ Amazing Benefits
Pride: Good and Bad
Temptation: 50+ Tips

Missions
Jim Elliot: Recorded Messages

Watch for more at www.booksrlr.com.

Table of Contents

NOTES: [1] For consistency and clarity, names and pronouns of God have been capitalized throughout including in Bible versions which do not follow that practice. [2] The author capitalizes three other words: "Word" when speaking of God's Word; "Church" when speaking of the Church universal; and "Cross" when referring to the Cross of Calvary. [3] *Italicized* words and [bracketed words] in Scripture have been added by the author. [4] The author does not abbreviate the names of Bible books since abbreviations can be unknown to some readers. [5] The author chooses to use a lot of Scripture quotations based on his belief that the Word of God and the Spirit of God are the two dominant factors in changing lives and growing the lives of Christians.

We hope you enjoy this book. Robert Lloyd Russell's goal is to provide high-quality, thought-provoking books that connect truth to real life needs and challenges. For more information on his other books based on Biblical interpretation and application, please visit his author's website booksrlr.

If you find value in this book, please consider writing an online review. The author would be grateful.

We hope you enjoy this book. Robert Lloyd Russell's goal is to provide high-quality, thought-provoking books that connect truth to real life needs and challenges. For more information on his other books based on Biblical interpretation and application, please visit his author's website https://booksrlr.com/

If you find value in this book, please consider writing an online review. This would be very much appreciated by the author.

> *Don't be selfish; don't try to impress others.*
> *Be humble, thinking of others*
> *as better than yourselves.*
> Philippians 2:3

Examples of Reader Responses

The writings of Robert Lloyd Russell have received a warm reception by a wide variety of people as seen in the quotes below. His books have received 11 national and international literary awards.

||||| |||||

☆☆☆☆☆ "He writes clearly so that the material is easily understood by both clergy and laity... Very edifying to read." ~ *William J. Petersen: Emeritus Senior Acquisitions Editor for Baker Book House and Fleming H. Revell.*

☆☆☆☆☆ "I loved the book... It is very well written and very understandable." ~ *Bob G., inmate*

☆☆☆☆☆ "I find it most inspirational... You make the reader think, and that is a great talent." ~ *Evelyn Cox, homemaker*

☆☆☆☆☆ "First there was Tozer with "*The Knowledge of the Holy,*" and then Packer gave us "*Knowing God,*" and now Russell has taken us further." ~ *Dr. Earl D. Radmacher, General Editor, Nelson Study Bible/New King James Study Bible* [regarding eBook "*GOD'S NATURE: Sonlight Sunlight*" / print book "*GOD LIGHT: Sunlight Sonlight*"]

☆☆☆☆☆ "The definitive work on Psalm 1:3. Mr. Russell has a tremendous gift for analogy. The most impressive thing is the way he has built off of existing undeniable Scriptural concepts. I am very impressed with his use of certain Scriptures, such as with regard to trees being deceptive in appearance... His work is very interesting, very clear, and intensely practical." ~ *Ronald B. Allen, Senior Professor of Bible Exposition, Dallas Theological Seminary* [regarding an early draft of "*GOD'S CHILD: Like a Tree*"]

5

Dedication

To

All God's Children

Who Recognize

Their Struggle

With PrIde.

1.

Why This Book?

"PrIde goes before destruction, and a haughty spirit before a fall. Better to be of a humble spirit with the lowly, than to divide the spoil with the proud. He who heeds the Word wisely will find good, and whoever trusts in the Lord, happy is he."

Proverbs 16:18-20

During the last several years I have used an automatic response to the question, "What is the next book you are working on?" My consistent tongue-in-cheek reply has been *"Humility and How You Too Can Obtain It."* The response is usually a chuckle and sometimes a skewed look at me.

Not only is the humor in the title immediately obvious to most, it also presents a profound truth: the moment you think you are humble you are showing your prIde.

This elusive quality of humility is humbling in itself. When you think you have achieved humility, it is really your prIde that you are expressing.

When I use the word prIde in this book, I use an upper case I to remind myself that at the center of every form of human prIde is the appropriate letter "I", since prIde is all about self-centeredness. If any short description exemplifies the culture of our day, it is self-seeking and prIde. There is, however, such a thing as good pride, which we also consider in this book.

This book is written by someone unworthy to write on the topic. But I believe it is a necessary topic to discuss and that God uses flawed servants to do His work.

While I realize that this book, or any other teaching, will not cure the human attribute of prIde, my trust is that the reader will be able to understand and appreciate the enormity of the problem of prIde in all of our hearts to a greater degree.

There is a huge dichotomy involved because the greater humility a person possesses, the more aware of their prIde and arrogance they become.

Charles Haddon Spurgeon, the Prince of Preachers, said, "That demon of prIde was born with us, it will not die an hour before us."

This book is intended to shine light on this tough area of our human nature as well as provide some practical tips for dealing with our innate prIde.

There is a story regarding Spurgeon. You may well be aware that he spoke every Sunday for many years to literally thousands of church attendees. Keep in mind that this was before the days of microphones!

The legend is that following one sermon he was greeting his parishioners as was his habit. One elderly lady said to him, "Charles Haddon Spurgeon, I want you to know that was the finest sermon I have ever heard you preach."

Without hesitation he responded, "Ma'am, thank you... but the devil already told me that."

A critical key realization is that since the Fall of Man in the Garden of Eden, prIde has been a part of every human being and will continue to be until our deaths.

Self is at the center of prIde and that reality is at the center of our English word prIde, the letter "I".

A core issue for dealing with prIde is the Cross of Calvary. If every morning as we rise for the day we would focus on the Cross and all its implications, we will reduce our arrogance significantly.

Another dichotomy of prIde is as Spurgeon put it, "PrIde is something that *should be* unnatural to us, for we have nothing to be proud of."

For example, to become a true believer in God and become one of His blood-bought children requires that you give up your prIde. It requires a recognition that you can do nothing to earn your way to heaven or to enhance your standing with God. The only way is to let go of your prIde and realize that Jesus Christ has done it all for you – "It is finished!" (John 19:30), our Savior's final words as His sinless life was presented to God His Father as payment for your sin and mine.

The reason why so many resist the call of Jesus Christ is that it requires giving up their false prIde in earning their way to heaven and instead accepting the free gift of eternal life offered by Christ.

All religions require that you DO something, whereas in Christianity it has been DONE for you. This, of course, flies in the face of our prIde-based nature that wants to earn our way to God's approval and entrance into heaven. Rather than a works-based *religion* Christianity is a faith-based *relationship*.

Issues

One of the problems with prIde is that it is very deceiving. Others can see the prIde in us, but we don't see the prIde in ourselves.

If you are thinking, I don't have a problem with prIde, then this book is especially relevant for you. However, it is very important reading for everyone.

Based on my own personal experience, I completely agree with whoever said "love is blind, but prIde is blinder."

PrIde will destroy your relationships with others, but humility is the best antidote.

Quotes

"You don't have to give up your intellect to trust the Bible. You have to give up your prIde." –R.C. Sproul

"A proud man is always looking down on things and people; and of course, as long as you are looking down, you cannot see something that is above you." –C.S. Lewis

"Christians are not so much in danger when they are persecuted as when they are admired." –Charles H. Spurgeon

Think and Grow

1. Is prIde an issue with you?
2. Has your personal prIde ever bothered you?
3. Has anyone ever told you that you are prIdeful?
4. Are you willing to work on reducing your prIde?
5. Do you know how to give up your prIde?

2.

The Origin of PrIde

"I will be like the Most High."

Isaiah 14:14b

The desire to be like, equal to, or greater than God stems from personal prIde. Yet that is the root of the fall of Lucifer from his angelic position in heaven.

The Historical Account

"How you are fallen from heaven, O Lucifer, son of the morning! How you are cut down to the ground, you who weakened the nations! For you have said in your heart: *'I will ascend into heaven, I will exalt my throne above the stars of God; I will also sit on the mount of the congregation on the farthest sides of the north; I will ascend above the heights of the clouds, I will be like the Most High.'* Yet you shall be brought down to Sheol, to the lowest depths of the Pit.

"Those who see you will gaze at you, and consider you, saying: 'Is this the man who made the earth tremble, who shook kingdoms, who made the world as a wilderness and destroyed its cities, who did not open the house of his prisoners?'

"All the kings of the nations, all of them, sleep in glory, everyone in his own house; but you are cast out of your grave like an abominable branch, like the garment of those who are slain, thrust through with a sword, who go down to the stones of the pit, like a corpse trodden underfoot. You will not be joined with them in burial, because you have destroyed your land and slain your people. The brood of evildoers shall never be named. Prepare slaughter for his children because of the iniquity of their fathers, lest they rise up and possess the land, and fill the face of the world with cities" (Isaiah 14:12-21).

What Happened?

God does not create evil. God created Lucifer as an angel with a free will, but He did not create him as Satan.

Lucifer forfeited the name God gave him and earned his new name of *Satan* (which means "adversary" or "enemy"). He did this by his own will (his choice). But how?

Lucifer was not living in a sinful world. He had no tempter to nudge him towards prIde. He didn't even have an innate sinful nature to overpower him (the Fall of Man had not yet occurred).

So we ask, how could prIde enter into an angelic being?

The answer lies in the simple reality that just like you and me, Lucifer was created with freedom to choose.

Each one of us also has been given choice. Our freedom to choose includes the opportunity to love God or rebel against Him. Lucifer chose to use his freedom of choice (given to him by His Creator) to rebel against the very God who had given him so much. Lucifer became proud, not of anything he had done but of the gifts God gave him. Lucifer wanted to be glorified. His was the first sin ever committed in the entire cosmos. This was the origin of prIde and since then, prIde has been a root of every sin.

As a result of his anointed role in the heavens and his great beauty, Lucifer's heart filled with prIde, and God cast him out of Heaven (Ezekiel 28:17). To this day Satan remains arrogant, prIdeful, and rebellious against God (Isaiah 14:12-14). It is a warning to us as

Christians that since Satan's personality is characterized by prIde, he will tempt us by using that same weakness in us.

The Core Issue

What caused Lucifer to fall from Heaven?

Isaiah 14:12-21 above tells us what happened to Lucifer's heart when he rebelled.

Lucifer's heart was captivated by prIde. He considered it not good enough to be an angel created in the beauty of God. Lucifer wanted to be equal with "the Most High."

Read the words of Jesus: "I saw Satan fall like lightning from Heaven" (Luke 10:18).

Sin [prIde] is always a heart issue and will eventually have tragic results.

The Bible warns us, "Keep your heart with all diligence, for out of it spring the issues of life" (Proverbs 4:23).

At the center of this is resistance to authority – any authority.

A few decades ago it was common to see bumper stickers such as "Question Authority" and "Resist Authority."

We see the adoption of this philosophy today with many young people who rebel at the idea of *any* authority. Older individuals are also sometimes taken up with this concept. This explains in part some of the societal problems that the United States and many other countries are experiencing.

This wanting to be totally independent, self-reliant, and without responsibility has extremely deep roots in prIde.

We all need to learn that God is God and I am not!

The Irrationality of Pride

There are a variety of Hebrew and Greek words which are translated as "pride" in our Bibles. But the basic meaning in all of them is that a person has a superior attitude toward others.

There is one habit I have practiced for some years now. When someone asks me: "How are you?" I always answer, "Better than I deserve." This reminds me of my true position as a sinner saved by God's grace and hopefully causes the questioner to think a little. In fact, it has started many interesting conversations.

A related habit is upon rising each morning I spend a few moments reflecting on the Cross of Calvary, its cost to our Savior, and the blessings to those who have been redeemed. It helps reduce my innate prIde.

In summary, God wants us to be humble because when we are prIdeful we elevate and trust in ourselves.

Quotes

St. Augustine wrote, "It was prIde that changed angels into devils; it is humility that makes men as angels."

"The essential vice, the utmost evil, is prIde... It was through prIde that the devil became the devil. PrIde leads to every other vice. It is the complete anti-God state of mind." –C. S. Lewis

THINK and GROW

1. Read Chapter 28 of Ezekiel. What do you learn about the fall of Lucifer?
2. Have you ever been proud of a natural ability or a spiritual

gift given to you by your Creator?

3. What things contribute to those feelings of prIde?
4. Do you ever look down on others because their prIde is displayed differently than your own?

3.

The Origin of PrIde on Earth

A Perfect Earth

God gave Adam and Eve a perfect garden of paradise to enjoy. God has always been a relational God, and He endowed the first couple with free will to obey or disobey His one command of what not to do.

Free Will

When God created man He included the gift of choice, just as He did when He created Lucifer. This free will provided an opportunity to love, be jealous of, or reject their Creator.

"Robots do not love. God created us with the capacity to love. We cannot force others to love us. We can make them serve us or obey us. But true love is founded on upon one's freedom to choose to respond." –Billy Graham

What if your husband or wife or other loved one had no choice but to love you? Would that be the same as if they voluntarily chose to love you? As a relational God it is His desire that we *choose* to love Him, thus free will, the ability to choose.

Adam and Eve owed their very existence to God, Who created them and placed them in the Garden of Eden, where He walked with them and communicated with them.

But prIde entered in, and they wanted to elevate themselves to equality with God. An underlying factor, even if subconscious, is a belief that they deserved more than they had. Do you suppose that jealousy was a part of their original sin? After all, God was more powerful than they were! Are these not factors in human existence today?

Unfortunately, ever since Adam and Eve sinned, we all possess to some degree those same irrationalities ingrained in our personalities. While it is true that some hide it better than others, we all have prIde. We must understand it and learn to minimize it by learning to be more Christ-like, including gaining a degree of His humility.

The Early and Lasting Results

First Temptation

"Now the serpent was more cunning than any beast of the field which the Lord God had made. And he said to the woman, '*Has God indeed said,* "You shall not eat of every tree of the garden"'?" (Genesis 3:1).

The Initial Response – Obedience

"And the woman said to the serpent, 'We may eat the fruit of the trees of the garden; but of the fruit of the tree which is in the midst of the garden, God has said, "You shall not eat it, nor shall you touch it, lest you die"'" (Genesis 3:2-3).

Second Temptation – Creation of Doubt

"Then the serpent said to the woman, '*You will not surely die.* For God knows that in the day you eat of it your eyes will be opened, and you will be like God, knowing good and evil'" (Genesis 3:4-5).

Free Will – Bad Choice

"So when the woman saw that the tree was good for food, that it was pleasant to the eyes, and a tree desirable to make one wise, she took of its fruit and ate. She also gave to her husband with her, and he ate" (Genesis 3:6). PrIde took over and they wanted to "be like God" (verse 5).

The Initial Result

"Then *the eyes of both of them were opened, and they knew that they were naked*; and they sewed fig leaves together and made themselves coverings" (Genesis 3:7).

Initial Consequence

"And they heard the sound of the Lord God walking in the garden in the cool of the day, and *Adam and his wife hid themselves from the presence of the Lord* God among the trees of the garden" (Genesis 3:8). Their perfect relationship with God was broken. Shame entered in. The same is true today, when we sin our relationship is broken and we are ashamed of our actions. Fortunately, "If we confess our sins He is faithful and just to forgive us" (1 John 1:9). Relationship is restored.

God Still Desires Relationship

"Then the Lord God called to Adam and said to him, 'Where are you?'" (Genesis 3:9).

A Shamed Response

"So he said, 'I heard Your voice in the garden, and I was afraid because I was naked; and I hid myself'" (Genesis 3:10). This is what sin does. It produces fear and shame while disrupting relationship.

A Loving Offer to Come Clean

"And God said, 'Who told you that you were naked? Have you eaten from the tree of which I commanded you that you should not eat?'" (Genesis 3:11). God did not ask in order that He might gain knowledge, rather He lovingly offered Adam a chance to confess and restore relationship.

The First Blame Game

"Then the man said, '*The woman whom You gave to be with me, she gave me of the tree*, and I ate'" (Genesis 3:12). This is the pattern of sin: one sin leads to another sin.

Equal Opportunity

Now God gives Eve a chance to come clean. "And the Lord God said to the woman, 'What is this you have done?' The woman said, '*The serpent deceived me*, and I ate'" (Genesis 3:12). Like Adam, she plays the blame game!

The Consequences

Genesis 3:14-24 lists the consequences of what theologians call "The Fall of Mankind," or simply "The Fall." The effect of Adam and Eve's failures continue through their blood line to all mankind since. As a consequence, we live in a fallen world.

The Good News

Following the First Adam there came to earth the Second Adam (or Last Adam), Jesus Christ, Who is able to put our relationship with God back together. The four Gospels (Matthew, Mark, Luke, and John) present His story and the salvation that He procured for fallen individuals. Romans 5:12-21 offers a concise comparison between the Two Adams.

Note

There is a brief overview of the First and Last Adam in Appendix A.

The Core Issue

"Now the serpent was more cunning than any beast of the field which the Lord God had made. And he said to the woman, *'Has God indeed said,* "You shall not eat of every tree of the garden"?'" (Genesis 3:1). Christianity is a matter of faith and trust.

The spiritual battle that was waged in the Garden of Eden was the first skirmish in a spiritual war that continues to this day. One of Satan's chief strategies is to create doubt regarding the truth of our Creator. In effect, Satan is continually whispering in mankind's ears. "Has God really said that?" "Did God really mean that?" "Does God really exist?"

The Blame Game

The great evangelist Dwight L. Moody said, "I have had more trouble with D.L. Moody than with any other man who has crossed my path. If I can keep him right, I don't have any trouble with other people."

We love to blame things on other people when the problem is actually within us.

Application

"Since Adam in perfection could not keep himself in Paradise, how can his imperfect children be so proud as to rely upon their own steadfastness?" –Charles H. Spurgeon

This raises a critical area of concern which will be partially addressed later in this book. The global answer is to intentionally become more Christlike through such basic spiritual disciplines as Bible reading and study, prayer, fellowship with other Christians, and following Christ's example of serving others.

THINK and GROW

1. Do you sometimes have trust in things of which you do not have full knowledge and yet you move forward? If so, may I suggest that you exercise faith in many areas of your life.
   a. Take for example faith in the design and construction of a chair which you sit on. It is likely you do not have the engineering expertise to evaluate the design. You were not at the factory overseeing the quality of its manufacturing.
   b. Another example is the design and construction of a highway bridge which you trust to drive over.
   c. How about when you fly on an airplane? The complex systems, its manufacturing quality, its airworthiness, the training of the pilot and your trust they will not have a major health issue while you are in the air.
2. Can you make a list of other examples of how you have exercised faith in relationship to something of which you do not have full knowledge?

4.

The Contrast to PrIde

"Everyone who exalts himself will be humbled, and he who humbles himself will be exalted."

Luke 18:14b

The way of prIde is the default human way. The Son of God shows us the divine way:

"Let this mind be in you which was also in Christ Jesus, who, being in the form of God, did not consider it robbery to be equal with God, but made Himself of no reputation, taking the form of a bondservant, and coming in the likeness of men. And being found in appearance as a man, *He humbled Himself and became obedient to the point of* death, even the death of the Cross. Therefore God also has highly exalted Him and given Him the name which is above every name, that at the name of Jesus every knee should bow, of those in heaven, and of those on earth, and of those under the earth, and that every tongue should confess that Jesus Christ is Lord, to the glory of God the Father" (Philippians 2:5-11).

Spiritual Realities Are Counter-Intuitive

Jesus spoke this parable to some who despised others and trusted in themselves that they were righteous:

"Two men went up to the temple to pray, one a Pharisee and the other a tax collector. The Pharisee stood and prayed thus with himself, *'God, I thank You that I am not like other men* — extortioners, unjust, adulterers, or even as this tax collector. I fast twice a week; I give tithes of all that I possess.' And the tax collector, standing afar off, would not so much as raise his eyes to heaven, but beat his breast, saying, '*God, be merciful to me a sinner!*' I tell you, this man went down to his house justified rather than the other; for *everyone who exalts himself will be humbled, and he who humbles himself will be exalted*" (Luke 18:9-14).

Contrasts

Light and darkness are opposites. Life and death are mutually exclusive. Love and hate are diametrically opposed to each other. Likewise, prIde and humility are opposites – they do not mix well.

Consider this comparison between Lucifer and Jesus Christ (from an unknown source).

Lucifer	*Christ Jesus*
P – Put yourself first	**G** – Gift from God
R – Relax and enjoy yourself	**R** – Repent your old ways
I – If it feels good do it	**A** – Ask God for forgiveness
D – Don't listen to anyone	**C** – Care for the lost
E – Entertain yourself	**E** – Eternal salvation

Consider Quotes from Christian Leaders

Andrew Murray put it this way, "Humility is the displacement of self by the enthronement of God."

"PrIde is the oldest and most common of sins. Humility is the rarest and most beautiful of graces." –J.C. Ryle

"We fell through prIde, and God saved us through humility." –St. Augustine

"As God has two dwelling places: heaven and a contrite heart, so has the devil – hell and a proud heart." –Thomas Watson

"Hell is full of people who think they deserve heaven. Heaven is full of people who know they deserve hell." –Trevin Wax

What Is PrIde?

PrIde is difficult to define! A related problem is that as soon as you think you are rid of prIde, you are prIdeful.

Dustin Benge gives examples of how prIde is manifest. In each case he gives an example of a phrase which manifests that form of prIde.

1. Self-appreciation – "Look at me!"
2. Self-sufficiency – "I can do it!"
3. Self-glorification – "Don't I look great!"
4. Self-attention – "Listen to me!"
5. Self-validation – "I am right!"
6. Self-seeking – "Give me mine!"
7. Self-adoration – "Praise me!"

Most of us can identify with each of these examples.

The Scriptures say, "Don't be selfish; don't try to impress others. Be humble, thinking of others as better than yourselves" (Philippians 2:3).

PrIde vs. Humility

In a similar way to prIde, humility is hard to define. Perhaps this is part of the reason that it is so hard to cultivate. (There are many divergent definitions of humility available.)

We tend to think that humility is at the opposite end of prIde – and certainly to a large extent that is true. We become closer to true humility as we become more Christlike.

A common dichotomy is that true humility is passive and weak, but actually Christlike humility is powerful and useful.

We understand that we are to humble ourselves before God. But what about choosing humility in everyday life?

Consider the following chart from an unknown source.

PrIde	*Humility*
Focuses on others' failures	Realizes how far they fall short and have overwhelming sense of their need to grow
Self-righteous, overly critical, and fault-finding	Compassionate and forgiving
Looks at their life through a telescope but others with a microscope	Looks for the best in others
Looks down on those who aren't as 'spiritual' or 'committed' as they are	Seeks to win people, not arguments
Thinks they know who is truly proud and truly humble	Realizes only God knows a person's true motives
Thinks everyone is privileged to have them involved	Leaves the judgement of the heart in God's hands
	Thinks they don't deserve the opportunities that God gives them

Scripture

Jesus said, "Judge not, that you be not judged. For with what judgment you judge, you will be judged; and with the measure you use, it will be measured back to you. And *why do you look at the speck in your brother's eye, but do not consider the plank in your own eye?* Or how can you say to your brother, 'Let me remove the speck from your eye;' and look, a plank is in your own eye? *Hypocrite! First remove the plank from your own eye, and then you will see clearly to remove the speck from your brother's eye*" (Matthew 7:1-5).

A Key Reality

If you are human, you are prIdeful.

Great Christian leaders of the past have recognized prIde in themselves.

"I groan daily under a body of sin and corruption. Oh for the time when I shall drop this flesh and be free from sin!" –C.H. Spurgeon

"The prayer of a Christian is not an attempt to force God's hand, but a humble acknowledgement of helplessness and dependence." –J.I. Packer

One of the subtle disasters of prIde is that it says to others that they aren't good enough – that is the implication that they are inferior to you.

Quotes

"The razor blade is sharp but can't cut a tree; the axe is strong but can't cut the hair. Everyone is important according to his/her own unique purpose... Never look down on anyone unless you are admiring their shoes..." –Unknown source

"Pure Christian humility disposes a person to take notice of everything that is good in others, and to make the most of it, and to dimmish their failings, but to give his eye chiefly on those things that are bad in himself." –Jonathan Edwards

"Do not desire to be the principal man in the church. Be lowly. Be humble, the best man in the church is the one who is willing to be a doormat for all to wipe their boots on, the brother who does not mind what happens to him at all, so long as God is glorified." –Charles Spurgeon

THINK and GROW

1. PrIde and humility are quite opposite to each other.

      a. Which do you tend to choose?

      b. Why do you think this is the case?

2. Carefully review the above chart the compares PrIde and Humility.

      a. For each line item on both sides of the chart give yourself a score (1-10).

      b. Which one item are you willing to commit to improve?

5.

The Supreme Example

"And being found in appearance as a man, Jesus Christ humbled Himself and became obedient to the point of death, even the death of the Cross. Therefore God also has highly exalted Him and given Him the name which is above every name."

Philippians 2:8-9

"No one ever started so high and humbled Himself so low as did Jesus in His incarnation." —Steven Lawson

There is a constant theme throughout the New Testament regarding the humility of our Savior Jesus Christ.

His Heart

It is interesting that while on earth there was only one time when Jesus spoke of His own heart, and His statement then was, *"Learn from Me, for I am gentle and lowly in heart*, and you will find rest for your souls" (Matthew 11:29b).

One of the many dichotomies in Scripture is the concept that those who are poor in spirit are rich in God's eyes and those who are proud are spiritually impoverished.

His Actions

When my wife and I were outside the White House grounds, I jokingly remarked, "I think I'll give the President a call to see if he has time for coffee with us." On another occasion outside the fence of Buckingham Palace I quipped, "I'm going to call the Queen and see if she has time for a cup of tea with us."

Imagine if you will that you have actually been invited to Buckingham Palace for dinner with the Queen and many of the world's most influential people. You attend with great intimidation. When things are about to start, the Queen arises from her chair and begins to personally serve you and attend to your needs.

This is not the way of our world and its protocols. However, the King of Kings and Lord of Lords operates by a different set of principles.

We read in Scripture that following a meal, Jesus poured water into a basin and began to wash the disciples' feet and to wipe them with the towel with which He was girded. "Then He came to Simon Peter. And Peter said to Him, 'Lord, are You washing my feet'?" (John 13:6).

You can hear the incredulity in Peter's voice. All the disciples were confused to put it mildly.

"Jesus answered and said to him, 'What I am doing you do not understand now, but you will know after this'" (John 13:7).

The Lesson

"So when He had washed their feet, taken His garments, and sat down again, He said to them, 'Do you know what I have done to you? You call Me Teacher and Lord, and you say well, for so I am. If I then, your Lord and Teacher, have washed your feet, you also ought to wash one another's feet. For I have given you an example, that you should do as I have done to you. Most assuredly, I say to you, a servant is not greater than his master; nor is he who is sent greater than he who sent him. If you know these things, blessed are you if you do them'" (John 13:12-17).

Application

It is not foot-washing that is the point, but rather meeting the needs of others in practical ways. In Jesus' day people walked or rode animals along dusty roads and cleaning feet regularly was a necessary thing.

Years ago my wife and I were on our way to a mid-week Bible study which we had been leading for years. Along the way we passed by the home of one of the couples who were faithful regulars in our group. We knew they were away on a trip to attend a memorial service for one of their parents. This time as we passed by their home, we saw another couple from our group cutting their grass for them. That is a modern-day foot-washing example.

Prayer

Without a servant attitude and mindset, our prayers are unlikely to be answered. In Scripture (Luke 18:9-14) we find that there was no answer to the proud Pharisee's prayer but God was attentive to the humbled tax-collector.

Jesus summed it up this way, "I tell you, this man went down to his house justified rather than the other; for everyone who exalts himself will be humbled, and he who humbles himself will be exalted" (Luke 18:14).

In other words, the way up is down!

Peter's Example

Simon Peter learned the hard way not to elevate himself.

Consider his denial of Christ. Where did it start? The answer is in the Upper Room, when Jesus told His disciples that one of them would betray Him and that He would be crucified, and furthermore they all would desert Him.

It was prIdeful over-confident Peter who exclaimed, "I will never desert You no matter what the others do!" (Mark 14:29 tlb). In essence Peter was saying to Jesus, "No way!"

So Jesus essentially told him, "As long as you brought it up, Peter, you're going to deny Me three times."

Scripture tells us, "PrIde goes before destruction, and a haughty spirit before a fall" (Proverbs 16:18).

Peter's downward step began because of a heart full of prIde. We know from Scripture that three times Peter did deny knowing Jesus.

The Bible warns us, "Keep your heart with all diligence, for out of it spring the issues of life" (Proverbs 4:23).

Application

Don't ever think that you can't fall. Every Christian is capable of falling to the worst sins imaginable. We want to keep as much distance from evil as possible because it's the small steps that lead to spiritual ruin.

The Supreme Example

"Let this mind be in you which was also in Christ Jesus, who, in the form of God, did not consider it robbery to be equal with God, but made Himself of no reputation, taking the form of a bondservant, and coming in the likeness of men. And being found in appearance as a man, *He humbled Himself and became obedient to the point of death, even the death of the Cross.*

"Therefore God also has highly exalted Him and given Him the name which is above every name, that at the name of Jesus every knee should bow, of those in heaven, and of those on earth, and of those under the earth, and that every tongue should confess that Jesus Christ is Lord, to the glory of God the Father" (Philippians 2:5-11).

Sometimes it's hard because of prIde to do what you know you should do, but you need to. When God sees humility, He honors it. If you are proud, forget about divine exaltation.

The Apostle Paul

Paul had many reasons to be proud.

"Then he [Paul] said: I am indeed a Jew, born in Tarsus of Cilicia, but *brought up in this city at the feet of Gamaliel, taught according to the strictness of our fathers' law*, and was zealous toward God as you all are today" (Acts 22:2-4b).

But God chose to use an affliction to humble Paul.

Paul tells us, "To keep me from becoming conceited because of these surpassingly great revelations, there was given me a thorn in my flesh, a messenger of Satan, to torment me. Three times I pleaded with the Lord to take it away from me. But He said to me, 'My grace is sufficient for you, My power is made perfect in weakness'" (2 Corinthians 12:7-9 niv).

Later Paul could say, "*I will not boast, except in my infirmities*. For though I might desire to boast, I will not be a fool" (2 Corinthians 12:5b-6a).

Quotes

"A mistake that makes you humble is much better than an achievement that makes you arrogant." –Unknown source

"The gift of humility is a rare virtue: embrace it!" –Balogun Iyanu

"When the people of God are near ripe for heaven, they grow more humble and self-denying... Paul had one foot in heaven when he called himself the chiefest of sinners and least of saints." ––John Flavel

THINK and GROW

1. The single most important question is have you humbled yourself before God and accepted the gift of salvation?
2. If not, why not?
3. If you have accepted the gift of salvation, are you living a life of humility?
4. If not, what intentional changes are you willing to make?

6.

Obstacle To Progress

"For by grace you have been saved through faith, and that not of yourselves; it is the gift of God, not of works, lest anyone should boast."

Ephesians 2:8-9

Have you ever been with a group where two or more people have argued over who gets to pay the check? How about when someone bought you coffee and as you parted you said, "Next time it's on me." We want to do our part and that is good except when it is impossible to do so.

Root Issue

God is the Creator. God is also a hard worker. We are made in God's image. Part of our humanity is to work hard and create things. Only humans use technology of various kinds. We are "made in the image of God" (Genesis 1:27, 9:6) and so we too are creators as well as doers.

The fact that religions require human effort and achievement appeals to man's natural instincts – and especially to our innate prIde, they are attractive to man. Christianity is a relationship rather than a religion, and that is not appealing to man's prIde. Religions are based on human effort whereas Christianity is based on what Christ has already done through His humility and obedience to His Father.

As noted throughout this book, our natural condition since the fall in the Garden of Eden is prIde. The more *we* accomplish the better we feel about ourselves. But too much continued success can easily cause an arrogance.

It was multi-billionaire Bill Gates who said, "Success is a lousy teacher, it seduces smart people into thinking they can't lose."

May I suggest that those of us with perfectionism tendencies may in many circumstances be particularly susceptible to prIde.

The Spiritual World

In spiritual things everything is reversed. "PrIde is the greatest stumbling block to spiritual progress." –T.I. Loveday

Fortunately, God has made provision for His people—the indwelling Spirit of God living within the believer.

Scripture

There are many warnings about prIde throughout the Word of God. Proverbs, a book of wisdom says, "PrIde goes before destruction, and haughtiness before a fall" (Proverbs 16:18).

Earlier in the Book of Proverbs is a well-known verse. Ponder it from various translations.

"Too much prIde can put you to shame. It's wiser to be humble" (Proverbs 11:2 cev).

"PrIde leads to disgrace, but with humility comes wisdom" (Proverbs 11:2 nlt).

"When prIde comes, then comes shame; but with the humble is wisdom" (Proverbs 11:2 nkjv).

"When prIde comes, then comes disgrace, but with the humble is wisdom" (Proverbs 11:2 esv).

"When prIde comes, then comes disgrace, but with humility comes wisdom" (Proverbs 11:2 niv).

"The stuck-up fall flat on their faces, but down-to-earth people stand firm" (Proverbs 11:2 msg).

One way of looking at this passage is that prIde is the first step down!

These versions are all saying that prIde brings a fall leading to failure whereas wisdom is a far better option. The opposite of wisdom, prIde, is foolishness!

The Solution

Jesus promised, "The Helper, the Holy Spirit, whom the Father will send in My name, He will teach you all things, and bring to your remembrance all things that I said to you" (John 14:26).

"But you are not in the flesh but in the Spirit, if indeed *the Spirit of God dwells in you*. Now if anyone does not have the Spirit of Christ, he is not His" (Romans 8:9).

"The Spirit Himself bears witness with our spirit that we are children of God" (Romans 8:16).

"Therefore do not be unwise, but understand what the will of the Lord is. And do not be drunk with wine, in which is dissipation; but *be filled with the Spirit*, speaking to one another in psalms and hymns and spiritual songs, singing and making melody in your heart to the Lord, giving thanks always for all things to God the Father in the name of our Lord Jesus Christ, *submitting to one another in the fear of [out of respect for] God*" (Ephesians 5:17-21).[1]

Our Natural Fruit

"Now *the works of the flesh are evident*, which are: adultery, fornication, uncleanness, lewdness, idolatry, sorcery, hatred, contentions, jealousies, outbursts of wrath, selfish ambitions, dissensions, heresies, envy, murders, drunkenness, revelries, and the like; of which I tell you beforehand, just as I also told you in time past, that those who practice such things will not inherit the kingdom of God" (Galatians 5:19-21).

Our Spiritual Fruit

... "But the fruit of the Spirit is love, joy, peace, longsuffering, kindness, goodness, faithfulness, gentleness, self-control. Against such there is no law. And *those who are Christ's have crucified the flesh with its passions and desires*. If we live in the Spirit, let us also walk in the Spirit. *Let us not become conceited*, provoking one another, envying one another" (Galatians 5:22-26).

Fruit Summary

Humility like this is one of the strongest evidences of the indwelling of the Spirit of God. We know nothing of humility by nature, for *we are all born proud.* To convince us of sin, to show us our own vileness and corruption, to put us in our right place, to make us lowly and self-abased – these are among the principal works which the Holy Spirit works in the soul of man. One of our Lord's sayings that is often quoted is the one which closes the parable of the Pharisee and Tax-collector — "every one that exalts himself shall be abased, and he that humbles himself shall be exalted" (Luke 18:14).

"To have great gifts, and do great things for God, is not given to all believers. But *all believers ought to strive to be clothed with humility.*" —J.C. Ryle

PrIde Prevents Salvation

Early in this chapter we referenced how hard it is for many to receive a gift with no strings or obligations attached – our prIde at work. Our human nature wants to be self-reliant, self-sufficient, and the "captain of my soul."

At an early age we find ourselves crying out, "I can do it on my own," or similar phrases.

We want justice but God offers grace. *Justice* is getting what we deserve and we want to prove our worthiness and then receive justice. *Grace* is getting something good that we do not deserve and we resist that since it flies in the face of earning our own way. In other words, prIde stands in the way.

We have a hard time accepting the grace of God, and His grace is the only way to escape the eternal horror of hell. God wants to, by grace, adopt us into His family, which includes an eternal home of utter completeness and true joy and happiness. God has given us the ability to choose that option.

Grace means that although we are unworthy to stand in God's presence as we are, He has chosen to adopt us into His royal family. Once we are adopted, when God the Father looks at us He sees His own sinless perfect Son Jesus Christ.

Salvation

When I accept God's grace, my sins are forgiven and I have the Spirit of God within me to help me grow like Christ. I now also have Jesus as my attorney sitting on the right hand of the Father (1 John 2:1), and a glorious future in heaven. Nothing can separate me from God from this point on.

The Apostle Paul said, "I am persuaded that neither death nor life, nor angels nor principalities nor powers, nor things present nor things to come, nor height nor depth, nor any other created thing, shall be able to separate us from the love of God which is in Christ Jesus our Lord" (Romans 8:38-39, check out verses 31-39).

THINK and GROW

1. Do you identify with the author's assertion that when someone does something good for us we immediately want to get even (i.e., even the score) rather than just graciously accept the gift?
2. Do you realize that it can be good to return something to those who have blessed you, but there is also often an element of prIde involved?
3. Do you truly recognize what an obstacle prIde is to your spiritual growth?

7.

Reality Check

"For the gifts and calling of God are without repentance."

Romans 11:29 kjv

What do you possess, including your ancestry, birthplace, natural abilities, spiritual gifts, or appearance that wasn't given to you by the Creator?

There is no room for feelings of superiority or for an inferiority complex.

Skill Sets

You have not created or provided anything regarding who you are. All has been given to you by the grace of God. *"Generous to a fault, You lavish your favor on all creatures"* (Psalm 145:16 msg).

It is an absolute truth that you are dependent upon God for your next breath. *"For the soul of every living thing is in the hand of God, and the breath of all mankind"* (Job 12:10 tlb).

You may have worked hard to develop skills you were given or you may have been lax in doing so, but the source of all is from your Creator. But you and I contribute or provide nothing – it all comes from God.

The best we can be is to be a distributor of God's blessings to others. It is our responsibility to use what we have been given by the grace of God for the glory of God.

"For all things are for your sakes, that *grace, having spread through the many, may cause thanksgiving to abound to the glory of God"* (2

Corinthians 4:13). "Whether you eat or drink, or whatever you do, do all to the glory of God" (1 Corinthians 10:31-32).

Paul understood these concepts.

The Apostle Paul

Paul had many advantages from a societal viewpoint. He used his great abilities effectively.

Chief Persecutor

"Then Paul said: 'I am indeed *a Jew, born in Tarsus of Cilicia, but brought up in this city at the feet of Gamaliel, taught according to the strictness of our fathers' law, and was zealous toward God as you all are today.* I persecuted this Way to the death, binding and delivering into prisons both men and women, as also the high priest bears me witness, and all the council of the elders, from whom I also received letters to the brethren, and went to Damascus to bring in chains even those who were there to Jerusalem to be punished" (Acts 22:2-5).

But God in His grace reached down to Paul and he saw the truth about God and about himself.

Chief Sinner

Paul could then say, "This is a faithful saying and worthy of all acceptance, that *Christ Jesus came into the world to save sinners, of whom I am chief.* However, for this reason I obtained mercy" (1 Timothy 1:15-16a).

Prosperity and PrIde

Good times can easily lull us into the neglect of God and into complacency and prIde.

"Yet I am the Lord your God ever since the land of Egypt, and you shall know no God but Me; for there is no Savior besides Me. I knew you in the wilderness, in the land of great drought. *When they had pasture, they were filled; they were filled and their heart was exalted; therefore they forgot Me*" (Hosea 13:4-6).

"I have been the Lord your God ever since I brought you out of Egypt. You must acknowledge no God but Me, for there is no other Savior. I took care of you in the wilderness, in that dry and thirsty land. But *when you had eaten and were satisfied, you became proud and forgot Me.* So now I will attack you like a lion, like a leopard that lurks along the road. Like a bear whose cubs have been taken away, I will tear out your heart. I will devour you like a hungry lioness and mangle you like a wild animal" (Hosea 13:4-8 nlt).

Nations

An unknown source has described the historical pattern of nations as follows:

..1 from <u>Bondage</u> to **SPIRITUAL FAITH**

.....2 from Spiritual Faith to **COURAGE**

........3 from Courage to **FREEDOM**

...........4 from Freedom to **ABUNDANCE**

...........4' from Abundance to **SELFISHNESS**

........3' from Selfishness to **APATHY**

.....2' from Apathy to **DEPENDENCY**

..1' from Dependency to **<u>BONDAGE</u>**

Students of the Old Testament will clearly identify with this cycle.

It is interesting to note that the average lifetime of nations is only about 200 years.

Individuals

This same pattern occurs very easily in individuals as well as nations. After great victories it is easy to slide backward even to the point of depression.

Here is a simplified version of this cycle:

.... Hard times create strong men.

.... Strong men create good times.

.... Good times create weak men.

.... Weak men create hard times.

Consider *Moses*, God's chosen emancipator and leader of Israel's thousands, yet he lost hope and asked God to kill him (Numbers 11).

The rugged prophet *Elijah*, who after triumphing over the prophets of Baal on Mount Carmel (1 Kings 18), ran away and curled up under a juniper tree, wanting to die.

Paul, too, the great apostle of grace, confessed that he "despaired even of life" while ministering in Asia (2 Corinthians 1:8).

Trouble Can Humble

While it is true that good times can easily lead to prIde, it is also true that bad times can lead to a more realistic view of ourselves and our abilities. It is good to be reminded of truth even if it comes through trouble.

Consider a clear example from the life of the Apostle Paul: "And *lest I should be exalted* above measure by the abundance of the revelations, a thorn in the flesh was given to me, a messenger of Satan to buffet me, *lest I be exalted* above measure. Concerning this thing I pleaded with the Lord three times that it might depart from me. And He said to me, 'My grace is sufficient for you, for My strength is made perfect in weakness.' Therefore most gladly *I will rather boast in my infirmities, that the power of Christ may rest upon me.* Therefore I take pleasure in infirmities, in reproaches, in needs, in persecutions, in distresses, for Christ's sake. For *when I am weak, then I am strong*" (2 Corinthians 12:7-10).

Only One Role Model

Charles H. Spurgeon put it this way, "Let us measure ourselves by our Master, and not by our fellow-servants, then prIde will be impossible."

THINK and GROW

1. Do you consistently remember that all that you are and all that you possess are grace gifts from God?
2. Have you like the Apostle Paul used some of your gifts for sinful activities?
3. Have you experienced an increase of prIde during good times?
4. Have you been driven to greater humility because of difficult times?
5. Contemplate the historical account of nations. Do you see this pattern happening in any current day nations?
6. Consider the similar pattern of individuals. Have you experienced parts of this cycle?

8.

Becoming Humble

"Humble yourselves under the mighty hand of God, that He may exalt you in due time, casting all your care upon Him, for He cares for you."

1 Peter 5:6-7

At the heart of the choice to humble ourselves is surrender. PrIde is in direct opposition to surrender. But our heavenly Father chooses or develops leaders for His kingdom from those who are willing give up their desires for His desires. [2] God wants servants who carry out their given leadership opportunities in accordance with His will. It always includes a willingness to die to self and our desires. It has everything to do with saying along with Jesus, "Not as I will, but as You will" (Matthew 26:39). This needs to be our approach in every area of our life.

The Critical First Step

The first step, C.S. Lewis says, is to realize that you are proud. If you don't think you are conceited, then you are very conceited indeed. The first step in humility is to recognize the truth of Scripture that you are a proud and arrogant individual (you might in fact work hard at concealing that from others but it is a fact).

In this first step it is helpful to remember, "In the sweat of your face you shall eat bread till you return to the ground, for out of it you were taken; for dust you are, and to dust you shall return" (Genesis 3:19). Be humble and recognize that you are no better than the next guy.

God gives grace to the humble because the humble are hungry for grace.

Recognize Your Blessings

"The mercies of God make a sinner proud, but a saint humble."
—Thomas Watson

"While others are congratulating themselves, I have to sit humbly at the foot of the Cross and marvel that I'm saved at all." —Charles Spurgeon

"Any real knowledge of Jesus Christ will knock all the prIde out of a person and bring him or her down in lowliness before His feet." —A.W. Tozer (*A Man of God*)

The Law versus The Gospel

Perhaps this is a key reason for the Law in the Old Testament. Scripture tells us it was and is a tutor for us. Later, we find the fulfillment of the Law in One person—the man, Christ Jesus. The Gospel of Jesus Christ is the key.

"*The Law* is for the self-righteous, to humble their prIde: *The Gospel* is for the lost, to remove their despair." —Charles H. Spurgeon

A Consistent Principle

No one becomes a true believer without a recognition of the sin problem in their lives. This requires humility – the opposite of our human nature's built-in prIde. Unless a person realizes their need for a Savior, they will not accept the pre-payment for their sin by Christ's blood on their behalf.

This continues as a growing Christian. Just like you cannot begin the Christian life without humility, you cannot effectively grow in the Christian faith without humility. The Christian who is becoming increasingly Christlike will be low in prIde and high in humility.

"PrIde is the greatest stumbling block to spiritual progress." —T.I. Loveday

Serve Others

"Watering others will make you humble. You will find better people in the world than yourself. You will be astonished to find how much grace there is where you thought there was none, and how much knowledge some have gained, while you, as yet, have made little progress with far greater opportunities." —Charles Haddon Spurgeon

Requirement for Progress

"The focus of health in the soul is humility, while the root of inward corruption is prIde. In the spiritual life, nothing stands still. If we are not constantly growing downward into humility, we shall be steadily swelling up and running to seed under the influence of prIde." —J.I. Packer

Summary

"Humble yourselves ... under the mighty hand of God so that at the proper time He may exalt you" (1 Peter 5:6). Exaltation is God's business; humble obedience is our responsibility.

Listen to the Apostle Paul

"I, therefore, the prisoner of the Lord, beseech you to *walk worthy of the calling* with which you were called, *with all lowliness and gentleness,* with longsuffering, bearing with one another in love, endeavoring to keep the unity of the Spirit in the bond of peace. There is one body and one Spirit, just as you were called in one hope of your calling; one Lord, one faith, one baptism; one God and Father of all, who is above all, and through all, and in you all" (Ephesians 4:1-6).

THINK and GROW

1. On a scale of 1-10 how would you rate your present humility? (1 equals the worst you have been and 10 equals your role model Jesus Christ.)
2. Are you satisfied with your rating? If not, what specific steps will you take to up your score?

9.

Be Humble or Stumble

"PrIde goes before destruction, and a haughty spirit before a fall."

Proverbs 16:18

"If you think you are standing strong, be careful not to fall."

1 Corinthians 10:12

"Every Christian has a choice between being humble and being humbled." —Charles Spurgeon

We sometimes read or hear about Christian leaders who fall into egregious sin. This rarely happens without warning signs. The typical progression is thoughts become attitudes, which develop into motivations, leading to actions. Actions often continue into a lifestyle.[3]

Using a tire analogy, major sin in a Christian life is rarely a blowout, rather it is almost always a slow leak.

"We should take heed of prIde; it is a sin that turned angels into devils." —Matthew Henry

"There is nothing into which the heart of man so easily falls as prIde, and yet there is no more vice which is more frequently, more emphatically, and more eloquently condemned in Scripture. PrIde is a thing which should be unnatural to us, for we have nothing to be proud of. In almost every other sin, we gather up ashes when the fire is gone. But here, what is left? The covetous man has his shining gold,

but what does the proud man have? He has less than he would have had without prIde, and is no gainer whatever. PrIde wins no crown."
—Charles Spurgeon

The Classic Example

Those who are familiar with the Gospels are familiar with the account of the Apostle Peter's denial of Jesus Christ. This is of such importance for us to understand that it is one of those rare events that is recorded in all four of the Gospels (Matthew 26:31-35; Mark 14:27-31; Luke 22:31-34; John 13:36-38).

Consider those humbling events in Peter's life.

"Then Jesus said to them [His disciples], 'All of you will be made to stumble because of Me this night, for it is written: "I will strike the Shepherd, and the sheep of the flock will be scattered"'" (Matthew 26:31). This came true following the crucifixion and burial.

"Peter answered and said to Him, 'Even if all are made to stumble because of You, *I will never be made to stumble.*' Jesus said to him, 'Assuredly, *I say to you that this night, before the rooster crows, you will deny Me three times.*' Peter said to Him, '*Even if I have to die with You, I will not deny You!*' And *so said all the disciples*" (Matthew 26:33-35). We see prIde and arrogance not only with Peter but with all the disciples. As sinful men, we underestimate our propensity to sin.

First Denial

"Having arrested Jesus, they led Him and brought Him into the high priest's house. But Peter followed at a distance. Now when they had kindled a fire in the midst of the courtyard and sat down together, Peter sat among them. And a certain servant girl, seeing him as he sat by the fire, looked intently at him and said, 'This man was also with Him.' But he denied Him, saying, '*Woman, I do not know Him*'" (Luke 22:54-57).

Second Denial

"And after a little while another saw him and said, 'You also are of them.' But Peter said, *'Man, I am not'!*" (Luke 22:58).

Third Denial

"Then after about an hour had passed, another confidently affirmed, saying, 'Surely this fellow also was with Him, for he is a Galilean.' But Peter said, *'Man, I do not know what you are saying'!*" (Luke 22:59-60a).

The Result

"Immediately, while he was still speaking, the rooster crowed. And the Lord turned and looked at Peter. Then Peter remembered the Word of the Lord, how He had said to him, 'Before the rooster crows, you will deny Me three times.' So *Peter went out and wept bitterly*" (Luke 22:60b-62).

Over-confidence has a way of catching up with us.

Three Critical Lessons

First, our failures are not a surprise to God. Jesus predicted Peter's three denials. God is omniscient (all-knowing) of the past, the present, and the future.

Second, "No matter how dear you are to God, if prIde is harbored in your spirit, He will whip it out of you. They that go up in their own estimation must come down again by His discipline." —Charles Spurgeon

Third, God is the God of second chances (and third, fourth, …). Peter became one of the most important leaders of the early Church. Note also that the Apostle Paul was a tyrant raging against Christians prior to his conversion and ministry. God wants you to look forward to the opportunities He has given to you rather than backward at your failures.

Your Future

One of my favorite hymns includes the words "Our times are in Thy hand; Father, we wish them there; Our life, our souls, our all, we leave entirely to Thy care." Think about those words for a minute! Would you desire anyone, but God, to be in control of your life?

But if we fully understand the truth of God's sovereignty in all things including our own lives, we are wise to consider the reality that "a man's heart plans his way, but the Lord directs his steps" (Proverbs 16:9).

Therefore, "Come now, you who say, 'Today or tomorrow we will go to such and such a city, spend a year there, buy and sell, and make a profit;' whereas you do not know what will happen tomorrow. For what is your life? It is even a vapor that appears for a little time and then vanishes away. Instead you ought to say, 'If the Lord wills, we shall live and do this or that.' But now you boast in your arrogance. All such boasting is evil" (James 4:13-16).

Observations

First, we must recognize that we have a responsibility before God to live carefully and safely and that it is God who allows events, including bad events, to enter our lives. Nothing should surprise us, and we have no idea how much longer God in His wisdom will keep us alive on earth.

Second, since we do not know what the future holds, we should make every moment count for God. The next verse in that passage reads, "Therefore, to him who knows to do good and does not do it, to him it is sin" (James 4:17).

THINK and GROW

1. Does that verse, "Therefore, to him who knows to do good and does not do it, to him it is sin" (James 4:17) cause you any concern?
2. Make a list of your recent sins of omission. Don't omit any of them!
3. The Scriptures record three times that Peter denied Christ. Make a list of times when you have denied your relationship with Christ (either directly or by not speaking up when the Spirit was guiding you to say something).
4. God is a God who provides future opportunities. Do you need to have a conversation of confession with God?
5. "Do not worry about how or what you should speak. For it will be given to you in that hour what you should speak; for it is not you who speak, but the Spirit of your Father who speaks in you" (Matthew 10:19b-20). Are you ready to intentionally follow the Spirit's guidance in the future?

10.

Service-Focused
Not Self-Focused

"Don't be selfish; don't try to impress others. Be humble, thinking of others as better than yourselves."

Philippians 2:3

Do you want to be great? If so, watch your prIde! But do you want to be great in the kingdom of God? If so, you will need to be humbled!

"Whoever desires to become great among you, let him be your servant. And whoever desires to be first among you, let him be your slave — just as the Son of Man did not come to be served, but to serve, and to give His life a ransom for many" (Matthew 20:26b-28).

"Jesus sat down, called the twelve, and said to them, 'If anyone desires to be first, he shall be last of all and servant of all'" (Mark 9:35).

The main goal of every serious Christian is to be more Christlike.

The World Needs Servants

The world needs people like Jesus, who "did not come to be served, but to serve" (Matthew 20:28). He chose prayer more than sleep, the wilderness over the Jordan, disobedient apostles over obedient angels.

Be A Provider

When there was no wine for the wedding guests, He supplied the best wine.

When the multitudes were hungry, He fed them.

When the disciples were afraid during a storm, He calmed the sea.

When the disciples had no money to pay taxes, He supplied it.

Jesus Christ met the needs of others as part of His servanthood.

Be Accessible

A woman with a disease interrupted His activities.

A woman in Samaria interrupted His day.

Another woman caught in adultery interrupted His sermon.

A person with remorse interrupted his meal.

Be Proactive

None of the apostles washed His feet, He washed theirs. When Jesus washed the disciples' feet, it was the greatest person to ever live on this planet revealing the character of God. He was a humble Servant.

None of the soldiers at the cross begged for mercy, yet He extended mercy.

His own followers scattered on Thursday, but He came searching for them on Sunday.

Be Uncomfortable

Often it is much more comfortable to sit back or do your own thing rather than to serve others. Jesus came to serve. You are to be like Him. Why not practice self-control by seeking every day to do something you would not naturally do? The heart of prIdeful man is seeking to do big things to become famous. But follow your Master and seek opportunities to serve others. Do small things in a great way as unto your Master.

The Explanation

"Jesus, being in the form of God, did not consider it robbery to be equal with God, but made Himself of no reputation, taking the form of a bondservant, and coming in the likeness of men. And being found in appearance as a man, *He humbled Himself and became obedient* to the point of death, even the death of the Cross" (Philippians 2:6-8).

As humans we often use our status for personal advantage. He used His position and power to serve others. On earth the premiere image of God is as a Servant.

He Kept His Power

He served and He knew His power came from God. We need to realize all of our power comes from God.

He Sought Approval

Jesus, the very Son of God, sought the continued approval of His Father through His obedience. We need to do the same.

Quote

"More than any other single way, the grace of humility is worked into our lives through the discipline of service... Nothing disciplines the inordinate desires of the flesh like service, and nothing transforms the desires of the flesh like serving in hiddenness. The flesh whines against service but screams against hidden service. It strains and pulls for honor and recognition." —Richard Foster (*Celebration of Discipline*).

THINK and GROW

1. How is your service score?

2. Make a list of additional ways you could serve others.
    a. In your local church.
    b. In your occupation.
    c. In your neighborhood.
    d. In your extended family.
    e. In your home.

11.

Benefits of Humility

"Blessed are those who are humble; they will receive what God has promised!"

Matthew 5:5

When you humble yourself and realize just how much you need God, your life will change. When you surrender to Him, you then experience true freedom.

"By humility and the fear of the Lord are riches and honor and life" (Proverbs 22:4).

There are many benefits to living a life of humility. Here are just a few.

Receive Grace

Grace, as we have said, is the receiving of something good you do not deserve. "But He gives more grace. Therefore, He says: *'God resists the proud, but gives grace to the humble'* (James 4:6). ...

Distance From the Devil

... "*Therefore* submit to God. Resist the devil and he will flee from you" (James 4:7). ...

Near to God

... "Draw near to God and *He will draw near to you*" (James 4:8).

"There will be three effects of nearness to Jesus: humility, happiness, and holiness." —Charles Spurgeon

Great in God's Eyes

The Son of God said, "Whoever humbles himself as this little child is the greatest in the kingdom of heaven" (Matthew 18:4).

Exalted Status

"Humble yourselves under the mighty hand of God, that He may exalt you in due time" (1 Peter 5:6).

Intimacy with God

Some cynic has stated, "The more I get to know people, the more I realize why Noah only let animals on the boat."

But there have always been those who sought to put God first in all their activities. There are many examples in the Bible. These examples were all imperfect and they all messed up at times, but their hearts' consistent desire was to please God and as a result God honored them.

We are told that Enoch "walked with God 300 years" (Genesis 5:22; Job 1:1,3,8) and was "one who pleased God" (Hebrews 11:5).

Noah "walked with God" (Genesis 6:9). It is interesting to note that Enoch was Noah's great grandfather.

Abraham "was called God's friend" (James 2:23).

We are told "the Lord would speak to Moses face to face, as a man speaks with his friend" (Exodus 33:11).

Regarding David we read that "the Lord has sought a man after His own heart" (Isaiah 13:14; Acts 13:22).

The Apostle John was "the disciple whom Jesus loved" (John 13:23, 19:26, 20:2, 21:7, 20).

The important point to realize in these examples is that God does not choose favorites but He allows us to choose how intimate we will be with Him.

Choose Right and God Will Use You

"*The Lord has sought for Himself a man after His own heart*, and the Lord has commanded him to be commander over His people" (1 Samuel 13:14b).

"Enoch lived sixty-five years, and begot Methuselah. After he begot Methuselah, *Enoch walked with God* three hundred years, and had sons and daughters. So all the days of Enoch were three hundred and sixty-five years. And *Enoch walked with* God" (Genesis 5:21-24a).

If you are a believer then God has chosen you to do great things for Him – but are you making the right choices so He can use you?

"For you are a holy people to the Lord your God; *the Lord your God has chosen you to be a people for Himself, a special treasure above all the peoples on the face of the earth*. The Lord did not set His love on you nor choose you because you were more in number than any other people, for you were the least of all peoples; but *because the Lord loves you*" (Deuteronomy 7:6-8a).

What God told His chosen people is applicable to Christians:

"But *you are a chosen generation, a royal priesthood*, a holy nation, *His own special people*, that you may proclaim the praises of Him who called you out of darkness into His marvelous light; who once were not a people but are now the people of God, who had not obtained mercy but now have obtained mercy" (1 Peter 2:9-10).

"Behold what manner of love the Father has bestowed on us, that we should be called children of God!" (1 John 3:1a).

Humility Quotes

"The focus of health in the soul is humility, while the root of inward corruption is prIde. In the spiritual life, nothing stands still. If we are not constantly growing downward into humility, we shall be steadily swelling up and running to seed under the influence of prIde." —J.I. Packer

"Humility is perfect quietness of heart. It is to expect nothing, to wonder at nothing that is done to me, to feel nothing done against me." —Andrew Murray

THINK and GROW

1. How intimate are you with God? (1-10)
2. How could you improve your current score?
3. Are you willing to work at improving your intimacy with God?
4. 1 Peter 2:9-10 says that God chose you to be His witness on earth. On a scale of 1-10 how well are you doing?
   a. By your lifestyle?
   b. With verbal witnessing?
5. The author stated: The important point to realize is that while it is true that God does not choose favorites, He allows us to choose how intimate we will be with Him. Would you benefit from making different choices from now on?

12.

Tests of Humility

"But on this one will I look: on him who is poor and of a contrite spirit, and who trembles at My Word."

Isaiah 66:2b

Humility is such a strange thing. The moment you think you are humble you have proof that you are not! The ultimate oxymoron is *proud humility*. I would submit it is impossible to measure your own degree of humility; however, there are at least two indicators of humility.

The First Test: Vertical Humility

The first and foundational issue is how do you see yourself in comparison to God?

"Jesus Christ, who, though He was God, did not demand and cling to His rights as God, but laid aside His mighty power and glory, taking the disguise of a slave and becoming like men. And *He humbled Himself even further, going so far as actually to die a criminal's death on a Cross.* Yet it was because of this that God raised Him up to the heights of heaven and gave Him a name which is above every other name, that at the name of Jesus every knee shall bow in heaven and on earth and under the earth, and every tongue shall confess that Jesus Christ is Lord, to the glory of God the Father" (Philippians 2:5b-11 tlb).

God is God and you are not! When an individual truly understands this, they have passed the first test of what one might term vertical humility. Surprisingly, many in today's world have not yet come to this basic understanding.

"'For all those things My hand has made, and all those things exist,' says the Lord. 'But on this one will I look: on him who is poor and of a contrite spirit, and who trembles at My Word'" (Isaiah 66:2).

The Second Test: Horizontal Humility

How do you view others? Does it sometimes resemble the following passage? "The Pharisee stood and prayed thus with himself, 'God, I thank You that I am not like other men — extortioners, unjust, adulterers, or even as this tax collector. I fast twice a week; I give tithes of all that I possess'" (Luke 18:11-12).

It is amazing how in our prIde we look down on those who sin differently than we do!

Have you ever compared yourself favorably to someone else who was also made in the image of God? Have you ever been proud of your natural abilities or your spiritual gifts? How about your appearance? ... your education? ... the institution you earned your degree from? ... your status in life? ... your home? ... your family? ... your faith?

These tests might be considered horizontal humility.

You cannot have humility without love for God *and* for others.

The Proof

Do you truly and genuinely see others as more important than yourself?

"Let nothing be done through selfish ambition or conceit, but *in lowliness of mind let each esteem others better than himself*. Let each of you look out not only for his own interests, but also for the interests of others" (Philippians 2:3-4).

Do you rejoice with another who received an award you hoped to win?

Are you *genuinely* surprised when you receive honor from another?

On the other hand, if you do win an award, are you happy to realize they recognize how much you deserved it?

Quotes

"You are not mature if you have a high esteem of yourself. He who boasts in himself is but a babe in Christ, if indeed he be in Christ at all. Young Christians may think much of themselves. Growing Christians think themselves nothing. Mature Christians know that they are less than nothing. The more Christlike we become, the more we mourn our infirmities, and the humbler is our estimate of ourselves." —Charles Spurgeon

"To help prevent spiritual pride, let us remember, that we did not choose Christ, but were chosen by Him." —George Whitefield

The Key

"Then one of them, a lawyer, asked Him a question, testing Him, and saying, 'Teacher, *which is the great commandment in the law?*' Jesus said to him, 'You shall love the Lord your God with all your heart, with all your soul, and with all your mind.' This is the first and great commandment. And the second is like it: '*You shall love your neighbor as yourself.*' On these two commandments hang all the Law and the Prophets" (Matthew 22:35-40).

Jesus Christ came to earth in human form with all the human emotions and frailties that we have. He overcame the temptations, difficulties, and problems of living with sinful humans and yet He lived a sinless perfect life. He left us with this instruction which is the ultimate test of our humility:

"*A new commandment* I give to you, that you *love one another; as I have loved you*, that you also love one another. By this all will know that you are My disciples, if you have love for one another" (John 13:34-35).

THINK and GROW

1. How would you rate yourself regarding vertical humility? (1-10)
2. How would you rate yourself regarding horizontal humility? (1-10)
3. Can you honestly say that you would be very happy for someone who won an award that you hoped to win?
4. Can you honestly say that you love other people as much as you love yourself?

13.

The Be-Attitudes

"As He who called you is holy, you also be holy in all your conduct,
because it is written, 'Be holy, for I am holy.'"

1 Peter 1:15-16

While He was on earth significant portions of our Savior's words were recorded for all time. When Jesus Christ spoke the words that have become known as the Sermon on the Mount, it was the beatitudes portion that became what is arguably the most famous portion of this message.

The reason they are so memorable is that they are opposite of how we typically behave!

Be-Attitudes

The beatitudes are found in the Gospel of Matthew chapter five.

Matthew 5:2-3 ~ *"Then He opened His mouth and taught them, saying: Blessed are the poor in spirit, for theirs is the kingdom of heaven."*

Instead of being humble we naturally proudly reach for status, honor, power, and high places in the societies and kingdoms on earth.

"Jesus spoke a parable to them, saying: 'The ground of a certain rich man yielded plentifully. And he thought within himself, saying, "What shall I do, since I have no room to store my crops?" So he said, "I will do this: I will pull down my barns and build greater, and there I will store all my crops and my goods. And I will say to my soul, 'Soul, you have many goods laid up for many years; take your ease; eat, drink, and be merry.' But God said to him, 'Fool! This night your soul will be required of you; then whose will those things be which you have provided?' So is he who lays up treasure for himself, and is not rich toward God" (Luke 12:16-21).

"You say, 'I am rich, have become wealthy, and have need of nothing' — and do not know that you are wretched, miserable, poor, blind, and naked" (Revelation 3:17).

Matthew 5:4 ~ *"Blessed are those who mourn, for they shall be comforted."*

Instead of mourning we are seeking higher and higher levels of pleasure, in many instances even with substance abuse.

"But know this, that in the last days perilous times will come... lovers of pleasure rather than lovers of God" (2 Timothy 3:1-4).

Matthew 5:5 ~ *"Blessed are the meek, for they shall inherit the earth."*

Meek in Scripture denotes *strength under control.*

We prefer that others know how strong we are. We tend to wield our power as a display of power regardless of how many it may hurt. In this world's political system the more power you have the more you can conquer and inherit large territories on earth. This is often done with disregard for how many are hurt and even killed in the quest. This world is full of arrogant people, and if we are honest we would agree that we are personally arrogant at times.

"But know this, that in the last days perilous times will come: for men will be lovers of themselves, lovers of money, boasters, proud, ... headstrong, haughty" (2 Timothy 3:1-4a).

Matthew 5:6 ~ *"Blessed are those who hunger and thirst for righteousness, for they shall be filled."*

Are you as hungry and thirsty for spiritual gain as you are to fulfill your physical need for food and drink?

The Psalmist could say, "How sweet are Your Words to my taste, sweeter than honey to my mouth! Through Your precepts I get understanding; therefore I hate every false way" (Psalm 119:103-104).

The writer of Hebrews put it plainly, "For though by this time you ought to be teachers, you need someone to teach you again the first principles of the oracles of God; and you have come to need milk and not solid food. For everyone who partakes only of milk is unskilled in the Word of righteousness, for he is a babe. But solid food belongs to those who are of full age, that is, those who by reason of use have their senses exercised to discern both good and evil" (Hebrews 5:12-14).

Matthew 5:7 ~ *"Blessed are the merciful, for they shall obtain mercy."*

Instead of being merciful to those who have wronged us, we often demand justice, retribution, and sometime revenge – even against our brothers and sisters in Christ.

"Now therefore, it is already an utter failure for you that you go to law against one another. Why do you not rather accept wrong? Why do you not rather let yourselves be cheated? No, you yourselves do wrong and cheat, and you do these things to your brethren!" (1 Corinthians 6:7-8).

Matthew 5:8 ~ *"Blessed are the pure in heart, for they shall see God."*

Our hearts are selfish, prIdeful, and seek personal satisfaction. Later in this Sermon on the Mount our Savior referenced how corrupt our hearts can be when left unchecked.

"You have heard that it was said to those of old, 'You shall not commit adultery.' But I say to you that whoever looks at a woman to lust for her has already committed adultery with her in his heart" (Matthew 5:27-28).

"Keep your heart with all diligence, for out of it spring the issues of life" (Proverbs 4:23).

Matthew 5:9 ~ *"Blessed are the peacemakers, for they shall be called sons of God."*

Our fallen tendency is to argue for what we think is correct. Often we become resentful of those who disagree with us, leading to quarrels.

"Do not grieve the Holy Spirit of God, by whom you were sealed for the day of redemption. Let all bitterness, wrath, anger, clamor, and evil speaking be put away from you, with all malice. And be kind to one another, tenderhearted, forgiving one another, even as God in Christ forgave you" (Ephesians 4:30-32).

Matthew 5:10 ~ *"Blessed are those who are persecuted for righteousness' sake, for theirs is the kingdom of heaven."*

We seek to avoid any kind of mistreatment – even if we know we are avoiding what God wants us to do. When we believe we are persecuted, our fallen reaction is to fight back in every way we are able.

"Jesus answered and said, 'Assuredly, I say to you, there is no one who has left house or brothers or sisters or father or mother or wife or children or lands, for My sake and the gospel's, who shall not receive a hundredfold now in this time — houses and brothers and sisters and mothers and children and lands, with persecutions — and in the age to come, eternal life. But many who are first will be last, and the last first'" (Mark 10:29-31).

Matthew 5:11-12 ~ *"Blessed are you when they revile and persecute you, and say all kinds of evil against you falsely for My sake. Rejoice and be exceedingly glad, for great is your reward in heaven, for so they persecuted the prophets who were before you."*

It is my personal belief that a major reason Christians are not the daily witnesses we are intended to be is that we fear any kind of rejection (which of course hurts our prIde).

Comment

Note that this passage known as the beatitudes contains statements about one who is becoming like Christ in their lives. One of the most critical traits of being like Christ is humility.

The more we learn about Christ, the more we will appreciate what Charles Haddon Spurgeon said, "Humility has been rightly said to be a correct estimate of ourselves."

THINK and GROW

1. Are you as hungry and thirsty for spiritual gain as you are to fulfill your physical need for food and drink? (Matthew 5:6)
2. Do you "hate every false way"? (Psalm 119:104)
3. When you have been slandered or falsely accused, do you feel blessed? (Matthew 5:11-12)

14.

Results of Humility

"A new commandment I give to you, that you love one another; as I have loved you, that you also love one another."

John 13:34

Decreased prIde and increased humility is an absolute core part of a Christian lifestyle that pleases God.

Quotes

"Real spiritual growth is always growth downward, so to speak, into profounder humility, which in healthy souls will become more and more apparent as they age." —J.I. Packer

"One mark of 'growth in grace' is increased humility. The man whose soul is 'growing,' feels his own sinfulness and unworthiness more every year." —J.C. Ryle

"Pure Christian humility disposes a person to take notice of everything that is good in others, and to make the most of it, and to dimmish their failings, but to give his eye chiefly on those things that are bad in himself." —Jonathan Edwards

A Clear View

The more humble a person becomes, the more he sees himself as God sees him.

"Why do you look at the speck in your brother's eye, but do not consider the plank in your own eye? Or how can you say to your brother, 'Let me remove the speck from your eye'; and look, a plank is in your own eye? Hypocrite! First remove the plank from your own eye, and then you will see clearly to remove the speck from your brother's eye" (Matthew 7:3-5).

We all need a correct view of ourselves. We all need to objectively consider what God sees in our heart and actions. While it is true God the Father sees us clothed with a white robe of righteousness because of Christ's payment for our sin, He is still all-knowing.

Under-Shepherds

"God is love" (1 John 4:8, 16).

Jesus' key instruction to His followers was, "A new commandment I give to you, that you love one another; as I have loved you, that you also love one another" (John 13:34).

If we are loving others, we will be tending to their needs and we will have unity with our brothers and sisters.

Witnessing

Not every Christian has the spiritual gift of an evangelist, but all believers are His representatives, His ambassadors for Him while He is away. Every Christian is to be a witness for Christ. A witness is only responsible to tell what they know firsthand.

Most of us find it easy to witness about a sports event, an opera, or even our children's sports, yet at times we seem incapable of speaking a good word on behalf of our Savior. God desires that we share with others what He has done, and is doing, for us.

"Sanctify the Lord God in your hearts, and always be ready to give a defense to everyone who asks you a reason for the hope that is in you, with meekness and fear; having a good conscience, that when they defame you as evildoers, those who revile your good conduct in Christ may be ashamed" (1 Peter 3:15-16).

When Jesus instructed us to love others as He has loved us, He made it clear in the next verse those actions in themselves will cause you to be an effective witness of the power of the Gospel of Jesus Christ.

"By this all will know that you are My disciples, if you have love for one another" (John 13:35).

He knew we should strive to have our walk match our talk.

The humble person is not afraid of rejection but is able to speak boldly for and about Christ.

Blessings

"God resists the proud, but gives grace to the humble" (James 4:6b).

Which do you prefer in your life? God resisting you and your efforts, or God's abundant grace in your life?

Summary

Jesus and humility are like a hand and glove. The way to please God is in humility which expresses itself in love to God and others—all others. When a humble person sees a down and out person, a criminal of the worst kind, or anyone different than themselves, they love the person even though they hate their sins—just as God does. The proud person, on the other hand, looks down on individuals because they sin differently than they do, or because they have overcome a particular sin which the other has not.

But the way Jesus lived, and taught us to live, is to have love for all.

"If you've gotten anything at all out of following Christ, if His love has made any difference in your life, if being in a community of the Spirit means anything to you, if you have a heart, if you care — then do me a favor: agree with each other, love each other, be deep-spirited friends. Don't push your way to the front; don't sweet-talk your way to the top. Put yourself aside, and help others get ahead. Don't be obsessed with getting your own advantage. Forget yourselves long enough to lend a helping hand" (Philippians 2:1-4 msg).

When you see yourself as God sees you, the result is a combination of confidence, kindness, love, and a servant's heart towards those around you.

The Bottom Line

It should be obvious by now that the biggest result of humility is that the more humble we become, the more we are like Jesus Christ our role model. That is the most important goal of any Christian and it is what most pleases our God and Father in heaven.

THINK and GROW

1. Are you reaping the benefits of humility? (score yourself 1-10)
2. Are you continuously growing more Christ-like?
3. Can you truly say you have true love for *all* others?

15.

The Second Worse Sin

"Everyone proud in heart is an abomination to the Lord."

Proverbs 16:5a

A couple of decades ago I began actively looking for a sin that does not have prIde at its core. So far, I have found none. PrIde was behind Lucifer's fall from heaven. PrIde was in the Garden of Eden with the desire to be like God. There is an element of prIde in every sin we commit.

"All sin is rebellion against God, all of it produced by prIde. PrIde seeks to dethrone God. It seeks to un-God God. It seeks to strike a fatal blow at His sovereignty and His majesty and to replace God with self. PrIde grips the sinner's heart." —John MacArthur (*The Mark of True Greatness*)

C.S. Lewis Quote

In the fall of 1942 C.S. Lewis gave his third series of talks that covered Christian behavior, including morality, sexual morality, forgiveness, faith, and "*The Great Sin*."

"There is one vice of which no man in the world is free; which everyone in the world loathes when he sees it in someone else and of which hardly any people, except Christians, ever imagine that they are guilty themselves. There is no fault which makes a man more unpopular, and no fault which we are more unconscious of in ourselves. And the more we have it ourselves, the more we dislike it in others.

"According to Christian teachers, the essential vice, *the utmost evil, is PrIde*. Unchastity, anger, greed, drunkenness, and all that, are mere fleabites in comparison. It was through prIde that the Devil became the Devil: *PrIde leads to every other vice.* It is the complete anti-God state of mind."

Recognizing that some in his audience would object, Lewis spent the rest of his talk giving reasons why prIde is the worst of all sins.

1. A proud person needs to be "better" than everyone else.
2. A proud person is never satisfied.
3. A proud person craves power.
4. PrIde makes you God's enemy.
5. PrIde makes you vulnerable to the Devil.
6. You can be blind to your own prIde.

God Hates PrIde

"Everyone proud in heart is an abomination to the Lord; though they join forces, none will go unpunished" (Proverbs 16:5).

"These six things the Lord hates, yes, seven are an abomination to Him: *a proud look* [the very first mentioned], a lying tongue, hands that shed innocent blood, a heart that devises wicked plans, feet that are swift in running to evil, a false witness who speaks lies, and one who sows discord among brethren" (Proverbs 6:16-19).

"Woe to those who are wise in their own eyes and clever in their own sight" (Isaiah 5:21).

"When prIde comes, then comes disgrace" (Proverbs 11:2).

It is no wonder that we also read, "I, wisdom, dwell with prudence, and find out knowledge and discretion. *The fear of the Lord is to hate evil;*

prIde and arrogance and the evil way and the perverse mouth I hate" (Proverbs 8:12-13).

The Second Worse Sin

There is an old saying, "Don't judge a person until you have walked a mile in their moccasins."

It is my personal belief that there is a base sin which must be in God's eyes the worst of all sins *for a believer*. It is spiritual prIde! Are you proud of your religious heritage? Are you proud of having the "right doctrine" compared to others? Are you proud of which denomination you belong?

What do you have... what have you experienced... what path have your travelled that wasn't in the providence of God?

Personal Anecdote – 1

Several years ago an incident happened which I have thought about many times since.

We moved into the first house in a new development. Some time later when a couple moved into their new house, they invited the neighbors for an open house. One of their fathers flew in from Minnesota. Somehow the new owner had heard that I was a pastor and introduced me to his father – who was a pastor – as also being a pastor.

His father's first question to me was, "What denomination are you?' I replied, "I am a Christian who happens to be attending a Baptist church." He was clearly startled and not sure how to reply. My sense was that he was very proud of his denomination affiliation and could not imagine why I responded as I did.

If I am correct in reading the situation, then spiritual and/or doctrinal position was a source of prIde to him.

It is my firm belief that what is critically important is a person's understanding of Christ regarding His birth, life, death, burial, and most importantly His resurrection. His resurrection puts the ultimate exclamation point on His divinity.

"If Christ is not risen, then our preaching is empty and your faith is also empty" (1 Corinthians 15:14-15).

Personal Anecdote – 2

In recent years as a Gideon in charge of church relations I have called upon a great many pastors. I have built strong relationships with many of them. Often when I am with a pastor that I know well and the time seems appropriate, I will ask the following question: "Do you ever wonder if when you get to heaven you will find out that some of your doctrinal positions are in error?"

I usually receive one of two reactions.

One response is an inquisitive look as they contemplate something they have not previously thought of.

The other response is one of horror – that I might think they are not completely doctrinally correct.

Which of these two do suppose has a root of prIde?

Quotes

"Spiritual prIde is the most dangerous and the most arrogant of all sorts of prIde." —Samuel Richardson

"Of all the pieces of prIde, this is the most dangerous, to prIde ourselves in our own righteousness." —Thomas Manton

"Many of us would agree that arrogant pride is one of the most repulsive of sins, yet little is spoken of it; and of those that have it, most will be absolutely convinced they don't. It is the simple sin of considering ourselves better than others, or thinking others less than us, but it can be very hard to see in the mirror. It can be spoken aloud, or be written in our eyes, but we can miss it for years. *It is one of the trickiest sins.* The Bible says it sets us up for a fall, leads to destruction, and is the sure mark of a fool.

"One of the clear messages of the Bible is the danger of pride. We see pride exhibited when place their own reasoning powers above the revelation of God and depend on their own finite minds to determine infinite truths. Pride was the original sin and has its place on God's hate list (Proverbs 6:16-19). King Solomon warns, "Pride goes before destruction, and a haughty spirit before a fall" (Proverbs 16:18). Indeed, God resists the proud in all their endeavors (James 4:6). —Dr. David Jeremiah (*I Never Thought I'd See The Day!*)

THINK and GROW

1. Why do you think God hates prIde so much?
2. How does prIde hurt your relationships with others?
3. How does prIde hurt your relationship with God?
4. The author quotes Proverbs 6:16-19 which lists some of the things at the top of the list regarding what God hates. The author has also stated that all sin has a root of prIde. Make a list of the seven sins in this passage bad how prIde is a root.
5. Consider the following C.S. Lewis quote in this chapter: "The more we have it [prIde] in ourselves, the more we dislike it [prIde] in others." Have you found this to be true?

16.

The Worst of All Sins

"Listen to this carefully. I'm warning you. There's nothing done or said that can't be forgiven. But if you persist in your slanders against God's Holy Spirit, you are repudiating the very One who forgives, sawing off the branch on which you're sitting, severing by your own perversity all connection with the One who forgives."

Mark 3:28-29 msg

God is a forgiving God. Take for example one of the thieves on one of the crosses beside Jesus Christ. He asked for forgiveness and our Savior's reply was, "Assuredly, I say to you, today you will be with Me in Paradise" (Luke 23:43).

Another example is the adulterous woman who was caught in the act of adultery by religious leaders. Jesus was not as concerned about her past as He was about her future. His words to her were, "Neither do I condemn you; go and sin no more" (John 8:11).

God is a God of second chances. In the account of Jonah who did the exact opposite of what God had directed him to do, God in His mercy gave him a second chance to obey God's instructions. "Now the Word of the Lord came to Jonah the second time, saying, 'Arise, go to Nineveh, that great city, and preach to it the message that I tell you.' So Jonah arose and went to Nineveh, according to the Word of the Lord" (Jonah 3:1-3).

King David committed adultery and murder. More importantly, he repented and followed his God and later we read that God declared David "a man after My own heart, who will do all My will" (Acts 13:22). Incredible!

God Is Patient With Us, To A Point

While we serve a longsuffering and patient God, there is a time when He will say in effect: enough is enough!

"The Lord executes righteousness and justice for all who are oppressed. He made known His ways to Moses, His acts to the children of Israel. The Lord is merciful and gracious, slow to anger, and abounding in mercy. *He will not always strive with us, nor will He keep His anger forever.* He has not [yet] dealt with us according to our sins, nor punished us according to our iniquities" (Psalm 103:6-10).

"And then *I will declare to them, 'I never knew you; depart from Me,* you who practice lawlessness!'" (Matthew 7:23). "Then He will also say to those on the left hand, 'Depart from Me, you cursed, into the everlasting fire prepared for the devil and his angels'" (Matthew 25:41).

The ONLY Unforgivable Sin

There is only one sin which the Word of God says is unforgiveable, the sin of rejecting the salvation which is found only at the Cross of Jesus Christ.

Failure to yield to the Holy Spirit's conviction of your need for a Savior will leave you unforgiven. Therefore, this is the worst sin anyone can commit – it is the only sin which guarantees you will not have eternal life in heaven with your Creator.

Heaven or Hell

In our modern society it is not politically correct to talk about hell. However, the Scriptures have a lot to say about the place called hell – the final destination of those who persist in this worst of all sin.

"The sacrifice of *the wicked [including any "good works"] is an abomination to the Lord,* but the prayer of the upright is His delight.

The way of the wicked [including self-effort to gain heaven] is an abomination to the Lord, but He loves him who follows righteousness. *Harsh discipline is for him who forsakes the way, and he who hates correction will die. Hell and Destruction are before the Lord*; so how much more the hearts of the sons of men" (Proverbs 15:8-11).

Jesus said, "Whatever I tell you in the dark, speak in the light; and what you hear in the ear, preach on the housetops. And *do not fear those who kill the body but cannot kill the soul. But rather fear Him who is able to destroy both soul and body in hell*" (Matthew 10:27-29).

Eternal Suffering

The choice is everlasting joy and happiness in heaven or everlasting pain and suffering in hell.

The only unforgiveable sin has a tragic result:

"Anyone not found written in the Book of Life was [will be] *cast into the lake of [unending] fire*" (Revelation 20:15).

"In the lake which burns with fire and brimstone, which is the second death" (Revelation 21:8).

Jesus described hell three times in short succession:

"Worm does not die and the fire is not quenched" (Mark 9:44, 46, 48).

THINK and GROW

1. Imagine a future date when you arrive at heaven's gate and you are asked, "Why should I let you in?" What would your answer be?
   a. Do you know what the only acceptable answer is?

    b. If not, keep reading and pay particular attention to Chapter 18 – Next Steps.

2. Can you think of any decision more important than this one?

17.

Important Realities

"I take pleasure in infirmities, in reproaches, in needs, in persecutions, in distresses, for Christ's sake. For when I am weak, then I am strong."

2 Corinthians 12:10

God has given each of us strengths but we are all prIdeful. It is only when you come to Him in humility, realizing that you cannot save yourself, that He will accept you into His family and give you everlasting life. Then God can use us.

God uses sinners with defects who have humbled themselves. Those who realize their dependence upon God become useful in His kingdom.

Biblical Examples

1. Aaron, Moses' brother – crafted a golden calf for the Israelites to worship.
2. Abraham   was old and fearful when God chose to use him.
3. David – committed adultery, arranged a murder, and had all kinds of family problems.
4. Elijah – was suicidal.
5. Gehazi, Elisha's servant – was materialistic.
6. Gideon – was poor, had low self-esteem and deep insecurities.
7. Isaiah – was a "man of unclean lips."
8. Jacob – was insecure and a manipulator.
9. Jeremiah – suffered from depression (appears to have had a *melancholy* or somewhat sad spirit).

10. John Mark – deserted Paul and Barnabas when they needed him the most.
11. John the Baptist – was eccentric.
12. Jonah – was reluctant and tried to run from God.
13. Joseph – had been abused before God used him.
14. Martha – was a worrier.
15. Moses – had a speech problem of stuttering, as well as a temper.
16. Paul – had an ongoing issue of "a thorn in the flesh" and may have been *choleric* (possessing a degree of irritability).
17. Peter – was compulsive, weak-willed, hot tempered, and denied the Lord during our Lord's most difficult time.
18. Rahab – was an immoral woman.
19. The Samaritan woman – had experienced several failed marriages.
20. Samson – was codependent and a notorious womanizer.
21. Solomon – chose self-indulgence over wisdom.
22. Thomas – was a doubter.
23. Timothy – was a timid person.
24. Zacchaeus – was very unpopular.

Key Point

Questions: Why did God use these flawed people mightily? Why can God likewise use you if you allow Him?"

Answer: God uses people who have failed, and do fail, because that is the only kind of people on earth!

Pre-requisite for God's Use

There is one critical factor for God to save you and use you. This far into this book you realize that the one pre-requisite is a significant amount of humility.

As Spurgeon put it: "Whenever God means to make a man great, he always breaks him in pieces first."

Can you honestly pray with Augustine: "O Lord, everything good in me is due to You. The rest is my fault."

Choose Humility

The humble person is a great person to be around. The arrogant person is typically a bore that people only like to be around or listen to because of factors that require them to maintain a relationship.

A prIdeful person tends to create division and strife. A humble person tends to bridge gaps and create harmony.

Take for example Moses. He did not exalt himself over others. He realized it was God who raised him up for a great task, not his own merit. He did not seek to be Israel's leader, rather it was a result of his obedience to what God was telling him to do. He kept his abilities, his position, and the task that God had given him in perspective.

"Then Miriam and Aaron spoke against Moses because of the Ethiopian woman whom he had married; for he had married an Ethiopian woman. So they said, 'Has the Lord indeed spoken only through Moses? Has He not spoken through us also?' And the Lord heard it. (Now the man Moses *was very humble, more than all men who were on the face of the earth*.)" (Numbers 12:1-3).

The Ten Commandments have been the foundation for civil society ever since Moses came down from the mountain with the tablets of stone.

It is interesting that the man who arguably was the most important man in history from the point of guiding mankind was the most-humble man on earth!

Moses did not seek to be Israel's leader, rather God elevated him to that position because of his willing and humble obedience.

Key Scripture

"The elders who are among you I exhort, I who am a fellow elder and a witness of the sufferings of Christ, and also a partaker of the glory that will be revealed: shepherd the flock of God which is among you, serving as overseers, not by compulsion but willingly, not for dishonest gain but eagerly; nor as being lords over those entrusted to you, but being examples to the flock; and when the Chief Shepherd appears, you will receive the crown of glory that does not fade away.

"Likewise you younger people, submit yourselves to your elders. Yes, all of you *be submissive to one another, and be clothed with humility*, for 'God resists the proud, but gives grace to the humble.'

"Therefore *humble yourselves under the mighty hand of God, that He may exalt you in due time*, casting all your care upon Him, for He cares for you'" (1 Peter 5:1-7).

Following this exhortation is this critically important warning:

"Be sober, be vigilant; because your adversary the devil walks about like a roaring lion, seeking whom he may devour. Resist him, steadfast in the faith, knowing that the same sufferings are experienced by your brotherhood in the world. But may the God of all grace, who called us to His eternal glory by Christ Jesus, after you have suffered a while, perfect, establish, strengthen, and settle you. To Him be the glory and the dominion forever and ever. Amen" (1 Peter 5:8-11).

The greater our prIde, the greater our susceptibility to our adversary.

Conclusion And Another Warning

God used imperfect misfits who were willing to humble themselves and seek God's direction for their lives. If this was true for Biblical characters, it can also be true for you and me.

But if you allow God to use you, never forget that sin is always a careless act away.

"Let him who thinks he stands take heed lest he fall. No temptation has overtaken you except such as is common to man; but God is faithful, who will not allow you to be tempted beyond what you are able, but with the temptation will also make the way of escape, that you may be able to bear it" (1 Corinthians 10:12-13).

There is a story which says that an elderly woman told John Newton she was sure that God chose her before she was born, for He never would have chosen her afterwards. I think there is some truth in that remark.

Quotes

Get rid of proud thoughts, for oh! what would they not do? PrIde dragged an angel from heaven, and made a devil of him, and prIde would drag any of us down to the level of the devil if we fall into its snare. God grant us grace to be rid of every proud thought, for we having nothing to be proud of." –C.H. Spurgeon

"When you feel yourself to be utterly unworthy, you have hit the truth." –Charles Spurgeon

THINK and GROW

1. Which of the imperfect Biblical characters listed at the beginning of this chapter do you most identify with?
2. Are you willing to let God use your weaknesses for the

benefit of His kingdom?

A Personal Note

I am a proud person. In contemplating the writing of this book I experienced much turmoil since I knew I am unworthy overall and especially to write on this subject. As the process of writing this book is nearing its completion, I am more aware than ever before how prIde infuses my entire life. My hope is that it will have some positive impact for eternity in the lives of some of my readers.

18.

Next Steps

"The Lord is not slack concerning His promise, as some count slackness, but is longsuffering toward us, not willing that any should perish but that all should come to repentance."

2 Peter 3:9

No matter who you are or what you have done or not done, God can use you. Not only that, God *wants* to use you!

Years ago my first sales manager told me something I have never forgotten. "Bob," he said, "Sales are really pretty simple. When you are with a prospect the first thing you do is to dig a pit and then throw your prospect into the pit. After they realize their predicament, you lower a ladder to them. At this point your prospect must accept the provision of the ladder that you offer. If they climb out, you have succeeded."

Your Most Important Decision

Have you settled your eternal destiny? Right this moment you are headed for either heaven or hell – there is no third alternative. Unless you make a deliberate decision, you are headed to an eternal punishment. If you are ready to receive the forgiveness and loving acceptance that Christ offers, it is simple:

Are You In The Pit?

Have you realized that you are a sinner? Do you agree with God's assessment?

"All have sinned and fall short of the glory of God" (Romans 3:23).

"What then? Are we better than they? Not at all. For we have previously charged *both Jews and Greeks [all of mankind] that they are all under sin.* 'As it is written: "*There is none righteous,* no, not one; there is none who understands; there is none who seeks after God. They have all turned aside; they have together become unprofitable; there is none who does good [in God's eyes], no, not one." Their throat is an open tomb; with their tongues they have practiced deceit;' the poison of asps is under their lips; whose mouth is full of cursing and bitterness. Their feet are swift to shed blood; destruction and misery are in their ways; and the way of peace they have not known.' *There is no fear of God* before their eyes" (Romans 3:9-18).

Do you believe you are included in these passages of Scripture?

Is Your Sin Bad Enough To Condemn You?

How many banks do you have to rob to be guilty of being a bank robber?

How many lies do you need to tell to be a liar?

How many sins do you need to commit to be guilty in God's eyes?

"For *whoever shall keep the whole law, and yet stumble in one point, he is guilty of all.* For He who said, 'Do not commit adultery,' also said, 'Do not murder.' Now if you do not commit adultery, but you do murder, you have become a transgressor of the law" (James 2:10-11).

"These *six things the Lord hates,* yes, seven are an abomination to Him: *a proud look* [have you ever been guilty of the first thing listed?], *a lying tongue* [any guilt?], hands that shed innocent blood, a heart that devises wicked plans, feet that are swift in running to evil, a false witness who speaks lies, and one who sows discord among brethren" (Proverbs 6:16-19).

Do You Realize The Penalty You Owe For Your Sin?

"The wages of sin is death, but the gift of God is eternal life in Christ Jesus our Lord" (Romans 6:23).

Are you, like me, hesitant to accept a free gift – feeling that you then owe the giver something? If so, I have good news for you. In exchange for the free gift – which comes without strings – it is God's desire that you learn more about Him through reading His Word (The Holy Bible), through prayer (becoming intimate with Him), through fellowship (enjoyment of friendships with other believers), and by serving Him.

"By grace [a gift of something good which you did not deserve] you have been saved through faith, and that not of yourselves; it is the gift of God, not of works, lest anyone should boast. For we are His workmanship, created in Christ Jesus for good works, which God prepared beforehand that we should walk in them" (Ephesians 2:8-10).

Dwight L. Moody once said, "I'm glad we are saved by grace, not by good works, because I don't want to sit in heaven and listen to everybody brag for eternity of how they got there."

Do You Recognize The Ladder?

Jesus said, "As Moses lifted up the serpent in the wilderness, even so must the Son of Man be lifted up [on the Cross], that *whoever believes in Him should not perish but have eternal life.* For God so loved the world that He gave His only begotten Son, that *whoever believes in Him should not perish but have everlasting life.* For God did not send His Son into the world to condemn the world, but that the world through Him might be saved.

"He who believes in Him is not condemned; but he who does not believe is condemned already, because he has not believed in the name of the

only begotten Son of God. And this is the condemnation, that the light has come into the world, and men loved darkness rather than light, because their deeds were evil. For everyone practicing evil hates the light and does not come to the light, lest his deeds should be exposed. But he who does the truth comes to the light, that his deeds may be clearly seen, that they have been done in God." (John 3:14-21).

Are You Humble Enough?

This is the bottom line: there are three questions you must answer!

First, do you admit that you have sinned?

Second, are you willing to admit your inability to save yourself?

Third, are you willing to accept the free gift of salvation and eternal life with God?

Summary

The process of salvation is as simple as A-B-C:

"**A**" ~ *Admit* that you have sinned.

"**B**" ~ *Believe* in the power of the resurrection of Jesus Christ.

"**C**" ~ *Choose* to trust Christ as your Savior and to learn of Him, seek to follow Him, and in so doing possess "the peace that passes any human understanding" (Philippians 4:7).

THINK and GROW

1. If you have not accepted Jesus Christ's offer of forgiveness and eternal life in heaven with Him, please consider the following:

a. Take a piece of paper and draw a vertical line down the middle. On one side write all the advantages of Christ's offer to you. On the other side list the advantages of continuing your current path.

b. Carefully contemplate this statement by Jesus Christ: "What profit is it to a man if he gains the whole world, and loses his own soul? Or what will a man give in exchange for his soul?" (Matthew 16:26-27).

2. If you need more specific help, I suggest you visit www.HeavenOrNot.net[1].

---

1. http://www.HeavenOrNot.net

19.

How To Reduce Your PrIde

"Whoever humbles himself as this little child is the greatest in the kingdom of heaven."

Matthew 18:4

If prIde is condemned by Scripture and believers are commanded to humble themselves, how can we accomplish that in obedience to our Savior?

Step One

Realize that you are not perfect – you are a sinner fueled by your own prIde.

Do you see how the "I" in prIde tends to control your life and is demonstrated by many "self" thoughts and statements?

Are you selfish? Even young children show their selfish nature. Small children say things such as, "Give it to me, it is mine." "I want it."

Do you love yourself in a prIdeful way?

How about preoccupation with your image?

Or, what about prIde in your career's accomplishments?

Do you think more about yourself and your desires as opposed to the needs of others?

Do you love yourself more than you love those around you? Have you evolved into self-worship?

Jesus said, "*A new commandment I give to you, that you love one another*; as I have loved you, that you also *love one another*. By this all will know that you are My disciples, if you have *love for one another*" (John 13:34-35).

As we have noted, prIde is a root of every sin! Are you aware of the prIde in your life?

Step Two

See yourself and others as God sees you.

Quotes from the Old Testament

"As it is written:

'There is none righteous, no, not one; there is none who understands; there is none who seeks after God. They have all turned aside; they have together become unprofitable; there is none who docs good, no, not one.'

'Their throat is an open tomb; with their tongues they have practiced deceit;'

'The poison of asps is under their lips;'

'Whose mouth is full of cursing and bitterness.'

'Their feet are swift to shed blood; destruction and misery are in their ways; and the way of peace they have not known.'

'There is no fear of God before their eyes'" (Romans 3:10-18).

The New Testament

"There is no difference; for all have sinned and fall short of the glory of God" (Romans 3:22b-23).

Step Three

There is a common saying that we should just pull ourselves up by our own bootstraps. If you have never tried to do that, do it now! Stand up and reach down and pull upward on your shoestrings.

Honestly now! How did that work for you?

We must realize that it is just as futile to get rid of prIde by our own effort. In fact, you will likely become proud of your progress in humility. Proud humility is quite an oxymoron.

As an individual Christian you cannot conquer prIde on your own. So how do we become obedient regarding humility?

The only answer is by relying on the indwelling Spirit of God to work in us. But this is not a passive activity. It takes intentionality.

"*Let us therefore be diligent* to enter that rest, lest anyone fall according to the same example of disobedience. For the Word of God is living and powerful, and sharper than any two-edged sword, piercing even to the division of soul and spirit, and of joints and marrow, and is *a discerner of the thoughts and intents of the heart.* And there is no creature hidden from His sight, but all things are naked and open to the eyes of Him to whom we must give account" (Hebrews 4:11-13).

God has provided us with everything we need to live in obedience to Him. It is our responsibility to access what He has provided.

"Grace and peace be multiplied to you in the knowledge of God and of Jesus our Lord, as *His divine power has given to us all things that pertain to life and godliness,* through the knowledge of Him who called us by glory and virtue, by which have been given to us exceedingly great and precious promises, that *through these you may be partakers of the divine nature, having escaped the corruption that is in the world through lust"* (2 Peter 1:2-4).

Notice the provisions are there – it is up to us to access them. What are the provisions? They are what are commonly called the "spiritual disciplines." Just like we need to discipline our physical bodies with proper nourishment, exercise, rest, and so forth, it is no different with our spirits.

Spiritual disciplines include regular time reading, meditating, and studying the Word of God. Regular prayer becoming intimate with God is another essential. Also vital is fellowship with other believers and some form of Christian service such as ministry in your local church and witnessing to unbelievers.

We all have the same 24 hours each day. It's a question of our priorities.

As you intentionally work on maintaining your spiritual life, you gain victory in your life including a lessening of prIde.

"Walk in the Spirit, and you shall not fulfill the lust of the flesh. For the flesh lusts against the Spirit, and the Spirit against the flesh; and these are contrary to one another, so that you do not do the things that you wish. But if you are led by the Spirit, you are not under the law" (Galatians 5:16-18).

"All Scripture is given by inspiration of God, and is profitable for doctrine, for reproof, for correction, for instruction in righteousness, *that the man of God may be complete, thoroughly equipped for every good work"* (2 Timothy 3:16-17).

One very important realization is that if you seek to honor your Creator, personal humility will follow. But humility does not mean you think of yourself as a doormat.

C.S. Lewis put it this way: "Do not imagine that if you meet a truly humble man he will be what most people call 'humble': he will not be a sort of greasy, smarmy person, who is always telling you he is nobody. Probably all you will think about him is that he seemed a cheerful, intelligent chap who took a real interest in what you said to him. *He will not be thinking about humility: he will not be thinking about himself at all.*"

Step Four

As you work towards true humility, you won't be preoccupied with yourself. You will only rarely be thinking about yourself and your needs. This is freeing and creates a joyful inner spirit. The secret is to seek God's honor in all we say and do.

A proper perspective regarding who we are and who God our Creator is, is a major critical factor. Placing yourself in right relationship with God will solve the problem of prIde. But this necessity is an ongoing activity.

As we honor God, humility will follow.

Summary

While God does not play favorites with His children, He allows each of us to decide how intimate we want to be with Him. The more intimate we become with our Savior, the more humility will characterize our lives.

Practical Tips

I once had a pastor who would frequently say, "Much prayer – much blessing. Little prayer – little blessing. No prayer – no blessing." While this is not a mathematical formula, it is a valid principle much like the sayings in the Book of Proverbs.

The key issue is to remain focused on God. There are so many distractions in our lives today we need to maintain perspective. One of my favorite verses follows:

"I, Nebuchadnezzar, raised my eyes toward heaven, and my sanity was restored. Then I praised the Most High; I honored and glorified Him Who lives forever" (Daniel 4:34a niv).

A practical idea is to ask specific people to point out prIde in your life whenever they see it.

Also, regularly count your blessings rather than your problems. This includes remembering your past, your milestones, when God has helped you in specific ways.

Danger Ahead

Some Christians believe they are so spiritually disciplined that they are above sin. Such a belief is not only wrong but is the utmost of arrogance. It also sets them up for a fall.

I believe that "spiritual prIde" of any kind must be the worst of all sins in God's eyes.

What natural talents or spiritual gifts do you take prIde in? Sure, you may have worked hard to improve your talents and gifts, but Who gave them to you? You were born with God-given abilities which you then developed.

"For *who makes you differ from another?* And *what do you have that you did not receive?* Now if you did indeed receive it, *why do you boast as if you had not received it?* (1 Corinthians 4:7).

PrIde is one of the deadly diseases, and one which destroys many preachers. God gives us spiritual gifts for His glory, not ours.

It would be good to commit to memory: "PrIde goes before destruction, and a haughty spirit before a fall" (Proverbs 16:18).

Quote

"There are many points and particulars in which the Gospel is offensive to human nature and revolting to the prIde of the creature. The Gospel was never intended to please man. How can we attribute such a purpose to God? Why should He devise a Gospel to suit the whims of our poor fallen human nature? He intended to save men, but He never intended to gratify their depraved tastes." –C.H. Spurgeon

Rewards

"The payoff for meekness and fear of God is plenty and honor and a satisfying life (Proverbs 22:4, msg).

Jesus said, "Whoever humbles himself as this little child is the greatest in the kingdom of heaven" (Matthew 18:4).

"*All of you serve each other with humble spirits*, for *God gives special blessings to those who are humble*, but sets Himself against those who are proud. If you will *humble yourselves under the mighty hand of God, in His good time He will lift you up*" (1 Peter 5:5b-6 tlb).

Think and Grow

1. How would you rate your average prIde (1 being very proud, 10 being always truly humble)?
2. Rate yourself from 1-10 regarding what percentage of your waking hours you are consciously aware of your proper relationship with God.
3. If your score is not as high as you would desire, what actions

are you willing to take to improve your score?

20.

Good Pride

"God forbid that I should boast except in the Cross of our Lord Jesus Christ."

Galatians 6:14

Not many people enjoy being around arrogant or boastful people. Such individuals tend to want to make others feel less significant than themselves.

Some Biblical commentators have distinguished three kinds of prIde found throughout Scripture. The typical list is something like this: a feeling of superiority, a feeling of being more dignified than others, and arrogance. No matter how you slice it whether in Hebrew, Greek, or English, in the Bible prIde has the connotation of a superior attitude or a belief that one is superior to others!

These may be useful categories, but what about good pride?

Is there such a thing?

All sin has a root of prIde – but not all pride includes an element of sin.

Wrong Boasting

"Come now, you who say, 'Today or tomorrow we will go to such and such a city, spend a year there, buy and sell, and make a profit;' whereas you do not know what will happen tomorrow. For what is your life? It is even a vapor that appears for a little time and then vanishes away. Instead you ought to say, 'If the Lord wills, we shall live and do this or that.' But *now you boast in your arrogance. All such boasting is evil*" (James 4:13-16).

But is there such a thing as good boasting? Yes, I believe that good pride is very definitely a reality.

Here are some Scriptures which present five examples of good pride.

Boast About God

"Indeed you are called a Jew, and rest on the law, and *make your boast in God*, and know His will, and approve the things that are excellent, being instructed out of the law" (Romans 2:17-19).

"For if the firstfruit is holy, the lump is also holy; and if the root is holy, so are the branches. And if some of the branches were broken off, and you, being a wild olive tree, were grafted in among them, and with them became a partaker of the root and fatness of the olive tree, do not boast against the branches. But *if you do boast, remember that you do not support the root, but the root supports you*" (Romans 11:16-18).

In 2 Chronicles, we read of how *Jehoshaphat's pride—his pride in God*—led to the removal of false idols: "Therefore the Lord established the kingdom in his hand; and all Judah gave presents to Jehoshaphat, and he had riches and honor in abundance. And *his heart took delight in the ways of the Lord*; moreover he removed the high places and wooden images from Judah" (2 Chronicles 17:5-6).

Warning

While pride in God is a good thing, it can also lead to a wrong kind of prIde. Be very careful.

Boast About The Cross

"See with what large letters I have written to you with my own hand! As many as desire to make a good showing in the flesh, these would compel you to be circumcised, only that they may not suffer persecution for the Cross of Christ. For not even those who are circumcised keep the law, but they desire to have you circumcised that they may boast in your flesh. But *God forbid that I should boast except in the Cross of our Lord Jesus Christ*, by whom the world has been crucified to me, and I to the world. For in Christ Jesus neither circumcision nor uncircumcision avails anything, but a new creation" (Galatians 6:11-15).

Warning

While pride regarding the Cross is a good thing, it can also lead to a wrong kind of prIde. Be very careful.

Boast About Others' Spiritual Growth

"We are bound to thank God always for you, brethren, as it is fitting, because your faith grows exceedingly, and the love of every one of you all abounds toward each other, *so that we ourselves boast of you among the churches of God for your patience and faith in all your persecutions and tribulations that you endure*, which is manifest evidence of the righteous judgment of God, that you may be counted worthy of the kingdom of God, for which you also suffer; since it is a righteous thing with God to repay with tribulation those who trouble you" (2 Thessalonians 1:3-6).

Warning

While pride regarding Christian activities and progress is a good thing, it can also lead to a wrong kind of prIde. Be very careful.

Boast In Weakness

"*If I must boast, I will boast in the things which concern my infirmity.* The God and Father of our Lord Jesus Christ, who is blessed forever, knows that I am not lying" (2 Corinthians 11:29-32).

"It is doubtless not profitable for me to boast. I will come to visions and revelations of the Lord: I know a man in Christ who fourteen years ago — whether in the body I do not know, or whether out of the body I do not know, God knows — such a one was caught up to the third heaven. And I know such a man — whether in the body or out of the body I do not know, God knows — how he was caught up into Paradise and heard inexpressible words, which it is not lawful for a man to utter. *Of such a one I will boast*; yet of myself *I will not boast, except in my infirmities. For though I might desire to boast, I will not be a fool*; for I will speak the truth. But I refrain, lest anyone should think of me above what he sees me to be or hears from me" (2 Corinthians 12:1-6).

"Concerning this thing I pleaded with the Lord three times that it might depart from me. And He said to me, 'My grace is sufficient for you, for My strength is made perfect in weakness.' *Therefore most gladly I will rather boast in my infirmities, that the power of Christ may rest upon me.* Therefore I take pleasure in infirmities, in reproaches, in needs, in persecutions, in distresses, for Christ's sake. For when I am weak, then I am strong" (2 Corinthians 12:8-10).

Warning

While pride regarding your weakness and dependence upon God is a good thing, it can also lead to a wrong kind of prIde. Be very careful.

Boast In God's Work Through You

"Therefore, knowing the fear of the Lord, we persuade men, but we are made manifest to God; and I hope that we are made manifest also in your consciences. We are not again commending ourselves to you but *are giving you an occasion to be proud of us*, so that you will have an answer for those who take pride in appearance and not in heart. For if we are beside ourselves, it is for God; if we are of sound mind, it is for you" (2 Corinthians 5:11-13 nasb).

"For *our boasting is this: the testimony of our conscience that we conducted ourselves in the world in simplicity and godly sincerity*, not with fleshly wisdom but by the grace of God, and more abundantly toward you. For we are not writing any other things to you than what you read or understand. Now I trust you will understand, even to the end (as also you have understood us in part), that *we are your boast as you also are ours*, in the day of the Lord Jesus" (2 Corinthians 1:12-14).

Paul writes of how he was giving the church in Corinth an occasion to be proud of him.

"For we do not commend ourselves again to you, but *give you opportunity to boast on our behalf*, that you may have an answer for those who boast in appearance and not in heart. For if we are beside ourselves, it is for God; or if we are of sound mind, it is for you. For the love of Christ compels us, because we judge thus: that if One died for all, then all died; and He died for all, that those who live should live no longer for themselves, but for Him who died for them and rose again" (2 Corinthians 5:12-15).

Warning

While pride regarding God's work through you is a good thing, it can easily lead to a wrong kind of prIde. Be very careful.

Arrogant Godly Pride?

Are these examples of arrogance? Examples of sin? No, *there's such a thing as godly pride. It's that pride that shines a light on God instead of man.* It's that pride that says, 'It's all God's. His gifts. His talents. His provision." It's the recognition that anything we can accomplish that is good for eternity is by God's power and grace.

Warning

PrIde is insidious. The moment you think you have reached a degree of humility, you have shown yourself to be prIdeful. Spiritual prIde must be totally abhorrent to God. In essence you are taking credit for His work. Be very careful to make sure that all pride is in respect to God and none of it is about you.

A Critical Difference

There is a huge difference between a desire for excellence versus a desire to excel.

I hate to admit it but there was a prIdeful time when I was working in the high-technology industry that does not make me feel good. It was a situation where I did not want to fail in a design that I was working on because I was afraid if I failed, the project would be given to one of the others in our group and he might succeed. That was my main motivation for persisting – to show my expertise and avoid another showing they could do something I failed at! At that point I was not so much interested in doing excellent work unto the Lord as I was motivated to excel over other engineers in the group.

While there is no call for being prIdeful about ourselves, there is a desperate need for Christians to take pride in their work. God not only wants us to do good works, He wants us to do good work.

Unfortunately, many Christians have confused sinful prIde about themselves with Godly pride in the work they are called to do.

At the other extreme there are cases where Christians accept mediocrity in their church out of subtle concern that striving for excellence would lead them into prIde. They avoid that temptation by settling for less than their best. What a perversion!

Our Lord of course strikes the right balance. He made the best wine and used it as a "sign" (which is what John's gospel calls it) that God's kingdom was coming in its fullness. Outstanding work is a signpost pointing to God because it manifests the goodness and overflowing excellence of God's kingdom.

A famous football player once said, "It's not bragging if you can do it." The fact is, *it's not bragging if you give God the credit—not just in public, but in your heart.*

Excellence and achievement don't give us bragging rights against others. Instead, Paul's command guides us: "Let the one who boasts boast in the Lord." We have reason to be proud of what we do in the high calling of our daily work, and reason to be humble, since "it is God who works in us both to will and to work" (Philippians 2:13).

"Do not glory in your own faith, your own feelings, your own knowledge, or your own diligence. Glory in nothing but Christ." –J.C. Ryle

The Bottom Line

The proud person views himself differently than God knows him to be.

It is prIde that causes us to trust in ourselves. A proud person believes that he or she can earn salvation or accomplish anything they want. Proud people believe that they can work their way up to God. In essence this is a slap in the face to God – as if His Son's sacrificial death on the Cross was not enough!

PrIde is really a heart issue.

PrIde seeks to promote self rather than God.

There is a problem: some confuse sinful prIde – all about themselves – with Godly pride in what God does and can do through His people.

"He [Jesus Christ, my Savior] must increase, but I must decrease" (John 3:30).

Excellence and achievement don't give us bragging rights over others.

Can you sincerely say to your brother or sister in Christ, "I'm so proud of you," when they've done something that honors God? What about when they received a reward that you had hoped to win?

"We should be lifting each other up and cheering each other on, not trying to outshine one another. The sky would be awfully dark with just one star." –Unknown

Never Forget

"Speak evil of no one, be peaceable, gentle, showing all humility to all men" (Titus 3:2).

"He who is greatest among you shall be your servant. And whoever exalts himself will be humbled, and he who humbles himself will be exalted" (Matthew 23:11-12).

"By humility and the fear of the Lord are riches and honor and life" (Proverbs 22:4).

The Key to Good Pride

John the Baptist understood our proper role on earth. He stated it in a simple statement:

"He must increase, but I must decrease" (John 3:30).

This is the absolute key for determining whether pride is good.

Think and Grow

1. Do you recognize aspects of prIde in your thinking?
2. Have you ever experienced "spiritual prIde"?
    a. Of your doctrine?
    b. Of your denomination?
    c. That you don't sin the way someone else does?
3. What action steps are you willing to take to reduce your prIde?

Appendix A
The First and Last Adams

"The first man Adam became a living being.

The Last Adam became a life-giving spirit."

1 Corinthians 15:45b

Most evangelical Biblical scholars agree that the first Adam was the fallen Adam of the Garden of Eden and the Last Adam is none other than Jesus Christ our Lord. Consider some thoughts regarding the two Adams—both similarities and contrasts.

Birth

The first Adam was created from virgin earth; the Last Adam came to earth through a virgin birth.

The first Adam was born without human parents; the Second Adam was born without a human father.

The first Adam was a creature representing God on earth; the Last Adam was God on earth.

The first Adam was created in God's image (Genesis 1:27). The Last Adam is the image of the invisible God (Colossians 1:15).

Life

The first Adam appeared on a scene prepared to receive him; the Last Adam entered a world ready to reject Him.

The first Adam was to receive the unqualified submission of all creatures on earth—he was to be lord of all. The Last Adam *is* the Lord of all even though He was rejected!

The first Adam's side was opened and a rib removed to make provision for his bride. The Last Adam's side was pierced by a Roman soldier's spear making provision (through His death) for His bride—the Church.

Due to the first Adam's sin, all mankind died. Due to the Last Adam's sinless life, all mankind is eligible for the forgiveness of their sins and to be made truly alive. When an individual chooses to accept Jesus Christ as Savior, he receives new spiritual life which never ends. This includes resurrection from death and eternal fellowship with the God of the universe.

Death

The first Adam introduced the Book of Death (1 Corinthians 15:22, Romans 5:12) which mankind since the Fall enters through natural birth. The Last Adam provides the opportunity for us to choose to enter the Book of Life through spiritual birth (Revelation 20:15, 21:27). The two Adams represent two distinct families currently on earth and in heaven.

The first Adam died spiritually in the Garden of Eden because of his sin. The Last Adam died physically in the Garden of Gethsemane for our sin (John 19:41).

The Crucial Difference

The response to temptation is a profound difference in the lives of the two Adams.

Most Christians are familiar with the three categories of temptation which are prevalent in our world. "Do not love the world or anything in the world. If anyone loves the world, the love of the Father is not in him. For everything in the world — [1] *the cravings of sinful man* [the base desires of the sinful nature], [2] *the lust of his eyes* [the desire for things] and [3] *the boasting of what he has and does* [prIde of accomplishment]—comes not from the Father but from the world. The world and its desires pass away, but the man who does the will of God lives forever" (1 John 2:15-17).

As we look at the first of these temptations–base desires–we find that Adam saw something that probably looked like good-tasting food (Genesis 3:6) and he ate of the forbidden fruit.

In the case of Jesus Christ, when Satan tempted Him to make a stone become bread, He refused and instead quoted the Word of God to Satan (Luke 4:4; see Deuteronomy 8:3). He had not eaten for 40 days (Luke 4:1), making the temptation very strong!

A second temptation which both Adams faced was visual. The first Adam saw that the forbidden fruit was "pleasing to the eye" (Genesis 3:6).

For the second time we see the opposite response from the Last Adam. "The devil led Him up to a high place and showed Him in an instant all the kingdoms of the world. And he said to Him, 'I will give you all their authority and splendor, for it has been given to me, and I can give it to anyone I want to. So if You worship me, it will all be Yours'" (Luke 4:5-7). Again, our Lord's method of dealing with Satan was to quote Scripture to Satan (Luke 4:8; see Deuteronomy 6:13).

Then we come to the third temptation. In the Garden of Eden we see Adam once again fall for Satan's temptations. The sin of prIde is a root of all sin and here it is very conspicuous. Adam saw that the forbidden fruit was "desirable for gaining wisdom" (Genesis 3:6).

For the third time we see the consistency of a life lived to please the Heavenly Father.

"Then the devil brought Him to Jerusalem, set Him on the pinnacle of the temple, and said to Him, 'If You are the Son of God, throw Yourself down from here. For it is written: "He shall give His angels charge over you, to keep you," and, "In their hands they shall bear you up, lest you dash your foot against a stone"'" (Luke 4:9-11). Christ refused and stood His ground by again quoting Scripture to Satan (see Psalm 91:11-12).

The first Adam had three temptations and gave in to each of them. The Second Adam had three temptations and refused to yield to any of them. A key lesson is that in each case Jesus Christ quoted the Word of God to Satan.

The Bottom Line

In Adam we got what we deserved, condemnation and guilt. In Christ, if we receive His offer of salvation, we receive what we don't deserve, grace and mercy (see Romans 5:12-21).

End Result

The story doesn't end in the Garden of Gethsemane. The Last Adam rose from the dead, victorious over sin on that first Easter morning, and is now seated at the right hand of the Father. One day, perhaps very soon, He will return for His Church.

Today two things are permanent on earth: (1) the sinfulness that mankind inherited from the first Adam, and (2) the Word of God, the Last Adam. "In the beginning was the Word [Jesus Christ], and the

Word was with God, and the Word was God. He was with God in the beginning. Through Him all things were made; without Him nothing was made that has been made" (John 1:1-4). Today God is working on earth through His Church, His bride.

About the Author

Robert Lloyd Russell

Biography

Robert Lloyd Russell's books have won national and international literary awards including a World Book Award (one of just three awards across all genres). He is the editor of a book containing transcribed spoken messages of martyred missionary Jim Elliot. As a small boy Robert lived in the Elliot home at a time prior to Jim's departure for the mission field. The transcriptions were carefully made from old wire recordings, the forerunner of magnetic tape recordings. Jim was one of Robert's Sunday School teachers and Jim's father was one of his spiritual mentors.

Russell has a diverse secular background which spans many functions including engineering, manufacturing, sales, marketing, and staff positions. His technical career included the management of a wide variety of engineers, physicists, and scientists in the high-technology industry.

During the 1970s while he was Camera Engineering Manager for a Fortune 500 corporation, he became fascinated with the attributes of light and the parallels to the attributes of God. He would later write about these parallels in some of his books.

In the early 1970s a senior executive of a major corporation began seeking Robert's opinions and advice. This was the start of a part-time consulting business. Then, from 1990 until his retirement in 2005, Robert devoted his entire career to advising and coaching many executives in a variety of organizations. Based in Portland, Oregon, his consulting practice routinely provided coaching and counseling on a wide range of business issues including ethics, overall effectiveness and profitability, organizational cultural issues, and Total Quality concepts.

During the 1980s as an active Christian businessman concerned about ethics, Robert enrolled in seminary and earned a Master of Christian Leadership degree from Western Seminary. For many years he was a popular adult Sunday School and Bible Study teacher.

His blog entitled "Abundant Life Now[1]" has been read in nearly 200 countries and translated into more than 110 languages.

Robert refers to himself as a simple **A-B-C** kind of guy: Christian **A**uthor, Christian **B**logger, and Christian **C**onsultant and **C**oach.

---

1. http://robertlloydrussell.blogspot.com/

Want Free Books?

As an author, I want to thank you for reading *SAMSON: Spirit-Filled to Self-Centered"* and I

regard the feedback of my readers very highly.

When considering buying a book many people weigh reviews carefully before deciding to purchase. If you enjoyed this book, would you consider assisting me by helping others make an informed decision? Leaving a review (even just a star rating without commentary) can help spread the message of the Gospel and increase others' faith through these books. It is also a great way to support this international ministry.

Robert Lloyd Russell's Newsletter[1]

Sign up for occasional updates from author Robert Lloyd Russell: https://www.subscribepage.com/rlr

He is committed to not bothering you with frequent newsletters. When he does send out occasional communications, it will contain one or more of the following:

- Advance information about current projects
- Related news
- Prayer requests
- Notification of **FREE eBooks** for a limited time
- Other items which may be of interest

---

1. *https://www.subscribepage.com/rlr*

(If you decide you no longer want to receive the newsletter, you may take advantage of the "unsubscribe" option at the bottom of each email.)

||||||

Robert Lloyd Russell's eBooks are available from your favorite online eBook retailer.

You may also want to visit the author's book website Books by Robert Lloyd Russell that lists his eBooks and printed books along with additional information, (booksrlr), or go to Books to Read[2] (https://books2read.com/ap/81Ym5B/Robert-Lloyd-Russell).

||||||

You are invited to connect with Robert Lloyd Russell through his daily internet blog *Abundant Life Now*[3] for inspiration and insight. (http://robertlloydrussell.blogspot.com/)

---

2. https://books2read.com/ap/81Ym5B/Robert-Lloyd-Russell

3. *http://RobertLloydRussell.blogspot.com/*

What To Read Next

"GOD'S NATURE: Sonlight—Sunlight" ISBN: 978-1393359371 ~ ASIN: B083L97PZV

An easy-to-read devotional style book which presents new and unforgettable insights. This landmark book identifies fascinating parallels between natural and spiritual light. Analogies teach profound truth in simple language.

"First there was Tozer with *The Knowledge of the Holy,* and then Packer gave us *Knowing God,* and now Russell has taken us further." —Dr. Earl D. Radmacher, General Editor, Nelson Study Bible/New King James Study Bible

Note: This eBook is an update of the first two sections of an earlier print book *GOD LIGHT: Sunlight Sonlight,* which **won six awards**.

Choose your favorite eBook retailer

https://books2read.com/GodsNature

"GOD'S CHILD: Like a Tree" ISBN: 978-1393518266 ~ ASIN: B0874CHLD7

Dr. Ronald B. Allen, a nationally recognized expert on the Psalms, described this book as "The definitive work on Psalm 1."

A timely book for those who long for faster, more consistent spiritual growth. In today's Christian communities many are complacent in their ultimate destination and they neglect the importance of the journey. In so doing, they miss out on many of the here and now benefits of their adoption into the family of God. The normal (not average) Christian is growing more like Jesus Christ as they continue their life on earth. If you long to be a disciple who pleases God, this book is for you. This book is extremely relevant to today's culture.

Choose your favorite eBook retailer

https://books2read.com/GodsChild

"GOD'S CHURCH: Christ's Pearl" ISBN: 978-1393268093 ~ ASIN: B07XFPMVQT

Early in the book the author provides a straightforward look at the three most popular interpretations of the parable of the pearl of great price. Included is a clear Bible-based rejection of the common notion that the pearl represents salvation.

The major portion of the work provides parallels between the "one pearl of great price" and the Christian Church. Presented are seven unique aspects of a pearl which parallel the uniqueness of the Church. Finally, eight additional characteristics of a pearl and their parallels are presented.

Note: This eBook is an update of an earlier print book *ONE PRECIOUS PEARL: God's Design for His Church,* which **won five awards**.

Choose your favorite eBook retailer

https://books2read.com/GodsChurch

"CHRIST'S DISCIPLE: How To Finish Strong" ISBN: 978-1393844402 ~ ASIN: B091XZF79B

Written for those who long for faster, more consistent spiritual growth. Many in today's Christian communities are complacent about their ultimate destination and they neglect the importance of the journey. In so doing, they miss out on many of the here and now benefits of their adoption into the family of God. The normal (not average) Christian is growing more like Jesus Christ as they continue their life on earth. If you long to be a disciple who pleases God, this book is for you.

Choose your favorite eBook retailer

https://books2read.com/ChristsDisciple

"GOD'S DESIRE: How To Please God" ISBN: 978-1393211785 ~ ASIN: B08H4F619W

This book develops two graphic models. The "Christian Life Model" is about victorious Christian living. Included in this section are the author's detailed acrostics for fellowship, obedience, power, prayer, witness, and the Word.

The "Christian Guidance Model" shows the interrelationship of the "Christian Life Model" and one's inner convictions, Godly counsel, and the Lordship of Jesus Christ.

Note: This eBook is an update of an earlier print book *"THY WILL BE DONE ON EARTH: Understanding God's Will for You."*

Choose your favorite eBook retailer

https://books2read.com/GodsDesire

"GOD'S LIGHT: How To Respond" ISBN: 978-1393424994

An easy-to-read devotional style book which identifies parallels between the reactions of physical objects to natural light and the reactions of humans to spiritual light. These analogies teach profound truth in simple language.

Written in short easily digestible segments, it is ideal reading for the person on the go. Readers gain a greater appreciation regarding Christians shining like lights.

Note: This eBook is an update of the third section of an earlier print book *GOD LIGHT: Sonlight Sunlight,* which won **six awards**.

Choose your favorite eBook retailer

https://books2read.com/GodsLight

"CHRIST'S BLOOD: 7+ Amazing Benefits" ISBN: 979-8201460877 ~ ASIN: B098W6LHVM

Understand the direct benefits to *you* from Christ's death and resurrection.

There are seven (plus one) directly stated benefits in Scripture.

Ponder ten additional benefits resulting from the Cross.

Choose your favorite eBook retailer

https://books2read.com/ChristsBlood

"TEMPTATION" 50+ Tips" ISBN: 979-8201564209 ~ ASIN: B0BCPN5YGW

Everyone is tempted (even Christ was)

50+ practical tips for personal victory over temptation!

Understand the battle and your spiritual weapons

Overcome the types of temptations you will face

Be confident and victorious in your Christian life

Choose your favorite eBook retailer

https://books2read.com/temptation-50tips

"PRIDE: Good and Bad" ISBN: 979-8201002053 ~ ASIN: B09SGSQLH9

Achieve a more consistent Christian life

As humans, we all have a common problem. Like rust to steel, pride is to our lives. Although there are examples of good pride in the Bible, most of the time pride is a negative part of our being.

Understanding the problem of pride is a vital part of gaining consistent spiritual victory as we live our daily lives.

Choose your favorite eBook retailer

https://books2read.com/Pride-Good-and-Bad

"*SAMSON: Spirit-Controlled to Self-Centered*" ISBN: 979-8215866122 ~ ASIN: B0BSZZSY8J

The Biblical account of Samson's life includes 10 significant victories interspersed among 15 problematic events.

How can we avoid a spiritually fickle life?

What are the commonalities and contrasts between the lives of Samson and Christ?

How did God evaluate Samson's life?

What practical lessons can we apply to our daily activities by looking at his life?

Choose your favorite eBook retailer

https://books2read.com/samson-robert-lloyd-russell

"*PETER: Failure to Faith*" ISBN: 979-8223422327 ~ ASIN: B0CBBC7DZC

Follow Peter's life in chronological order as he progresses from a fickle follower to a dynamic disciple.

This book can easily be a *fast read*. Due to small segments, it can also be used for *daily devotions* or in *short segments* by busy individuals. For scholars it can be the basis for a *lengthy personal study*. Small groups use it as a *spur to discussions*. Whatever your choice, enjoy as you read and reflect!

Choose your favorite eBook retailer

https://books2read.com/Peter-Failure-to-Faith

"JIM ELLIOT: Recorded Messages" ISBN: 978-1393887959 ~ ASIN: B088FZ3XSC

Note: This eBook is an updated and significantly expanded version of an earlier print book *"JIM ELLIOT: A Christian Martyr Speaks to You."*

Jim Elliot's spoken words transcribed for you – six practical messages with amazing depth and insight. These messages were given by this martyred Christian missionary before he left for the mission field in Ecuador. They were transcribed from a wire recorder, a forerunner of the magnetic tape recorder.

Christians of all maturity levels benefit from the understanding gained from Jim's discussions.

Choose your favorite eBook retailer

https://books2read.com/JimElliot

Print Book: ISBN: 978-0741475534 ~ ***"GOD LIGHT: Sunlight Sonlight"*** <u>won six awards</u> and is an easy-to-read devotional style book which presents new and unforgettable insights. This book identifies fascinating parallels between natural and spiritual light, and provides applications of natural and spiritual light. Analogies teach profound truth in simple language.

Available wherever quality print books are sold.

Note: There is an eBook update of the first two sections of this book entitled: *"GOD'S NATURE: Sonlight Sunlight."* The third section of this book is updated in the eBook entitled: *"GOD'S LIGHT: How To Respond."* Both are listed previously.

Print Book: ISBN: 978-0741462329 ~ **_ONE PRECIOUS PEARL: God's Design for His Church_**" <u>won five awards.</u>

A straightforward look at the three most common interpretations of this parable.

The major portion of the book provides parallels between the "one pearl of great price" and the Christian Church.

Available wherever quality print books are sold.

Note: There is an eBook update of this book is entitled "*GOD'S CHURCH: Christ's Pearl.*" It is listed previously.

Print Book: ISBN: 978-1606474310 ~ *"THY WILL BE DONE ON EARTH: Understanding God's Will for You"* is for those who are serious about living life in a way that pleases God.

Through the development of two graphic models the author provides insights regarding the interrelationship of fundamentals of the Christian faith.

Available wherever quality print books are sold.

Note: There is an eBook update of this book entitled *"GOD'S DESIRE: How To Please God."* It is listed previously.

Print Book: ISBN: 978-1615797646 ~ *"JIM ELLIOT: A Christian Martyr Speaks To You"* is directly relevant to all Christians.

Those with an interest in the history of missions or current missions will find the book riveting.

All Christians will appreciate Jim's straightforward, hard-hitting style of speaking.

Available wherever quality print books are sold.

Note: There is an eBook update of this book entitled *"JIM ELLIOT: Recorded Messages."* It has been enhanced and expanded with two additional messages and is listed previously.

[1] The author wrote a book based on this passage" "*GOD'S DESIRE: How To Please God¹*" (https://books2read.com/GodsDesire).

[2] A further study of God's desires for you is found in the author's book "*https://books2read.com/GodsDesire*" (https://books2read.com/GodsDesire).

[3] A further study of this progression is found in the author's book "*CHRIST'S DISCIPLE: How To Finish Strong²*" (https://books2read.com/ChristsDisciple)

---

1. *https://books2read.com/u/49M71J*

2. *https://books2read.com/ChristsDisciple*

Don't miss out!

Visit the website below and you can sign up to receive emails whenever Robert Lloyd Russell publishes a new book. There's no charge and no obligation.

https://books2read.com/r/B-A-QQUI-JGRVB

Connecting independent readers to independent writers.